TAX CUTS AND JOBS ACT FOR REAL ESTATE INVESTORS

THE NEW RULES

MICHAEL LANTRIP
Attorney | Accountant | Investor

TCJA FOR REAL ESTATE INVESTORS

THE AUTHOR

Michael Lantrip, Attorney at Law, is licensed to practice in Texas, North Carolina, Virginia, and the District of Columbia.

He has a B.B.A. in Finance from the University of Houston School of Business, and he has a Juris Doctor (J.D.) in Law from the University of Texas School of Law.

He is admitted to practice in all Courts in Texas, North Carolina, Virginia, and the District of Columbia, as well as the United States Tax Court, the United States Federal District Court for the Eastern District of Texas, and the D.C. Court of Appeals.

He is a member of the National Society of Accountants.

He practices in the fields of Tax Law, Real Estate Law, Corporate and Business Law, and Wills, Trusts and Estates.

MICHAEL LANTRIP

Formerly a Tax Examiner for the IRS, and a Tax Accountant for a Big 8 Accounting Firm, he has also been a Newspaper Reporter, Radio Announcer, Radio News Director, Television Reporter and Anchorman, Television Executive News Producer, and Military Intelligence Analyst.

As an elected County Attorney, responsible for Criminal Misdemeanor Prosecution, he handled over 2,000 cases.

In addition to 40 years of practicing law, he built one of the first computerized Abstract Plants and operated his own Title Insurance Company, becoming an Approved Title Attorney for seven national Title Insurance Underwriters. He has handled over 2,000 real estate closings.

As a Real Estate Investor, his activities have ranged from travel trailers to office buildings, and from on-campus condos to rural land.

Prior to his law career, he was a Radio Announcer at WQTE in Detroit during the "Motown" era, and he was a DJ at KIKK in Houston when it was named "Country Music Station of the Year" by Billboard Magazine.

He collects and refurbishes Vintage Audio Equipment.

He has written and produced over 1,000 half-hour Television Newscasts.

TCJA FOR REAL ESTATE INVESTORS

He has written over seven hundred stories as a daily Newspaper Reporter.

He has logged over 8,000 hours on the radio.

He is a Lifetime Member of Mensa.

He has been named a Top Writer by Quora.com where his Answers have been viewed more than 1,930,000 times.

He has written and published 9 books.

1.) "How To Do A Section 1031 Like Kind Exchange"

2.) "OMNIBUS EDITION How To Do A Section 1031 Like Kind Exchange"

3.) "50 Real Estate Investing Calculations"

4.) "Tax Cuts And Jobs Act For Real Estate Investors"

5.) "Your Best Business Entity for Real Estate Investing"

6.) "10 Other Real Estate Investments You Could Do"

7.) "Real Estate Investing Vocabulary Of Terms"

8.) "Section 121 Real Estate Investing System"

9.) "Do This, Not That!"

MICHAEL LANTRIP

All are available in digital and print at Amazon.

His Amazon Author Page is:

amazon.com/Michael-Lantrip/e/B01N2ZRGUY

His personal website is MichaelLantrip.com.

His Quora page is

www.Quora.com/profile/Michael-Lantrip-1

INTRODUCTION

Real Estate is enjoying the biggest growth cycle in thirty years after passage of the Tax Cuts And Jobs Act, and the big winners are the first Real Estate Investors to learn the new rules.

The IRS gift package includes:

- Lower personal tax brackets,
- 20% tax-free income for PTEs,
- 100% bonus depreciation for new and used property,
- 100% expensing of Section 179 improvements,
- Section 179 includes roofs, HVAC, fire and security,
- 40% lower Corporate tax rate,
- Elimination of Corporate Alternative Minimum Tax,

- A systemic lowering of Short Term Capital Gains tax,

- Doubled Standard Itemized Deductions,

- Property taxes are still deductible for businesses,

- Mortgage interest is still deductible for businesses,

- Extension of Retirement Plan loan repayment period,

- Doubled Estate Tax Exemption to $10M,

- Some relief from Alternative Minimum Tax, and

- Indefinite carryforward for Net Operating Losses.

The Real Estate Investing decisions that you made in the past will probably be the wrong ones to make this year.

For Example, the 20% income exclusion for PTEs now affects every real estate investing decision, and you need to understand how it works.

Bonus Depreciation is now 100% instead of 50%, and it includes used property as well as new property. If you are smart in using this new rule, you could double your cash flow.

TCJA FOR REAL ESTATE INVESTORS

The 100% expensing of Section 179 improvements, and the addition of roofs, HVAC, and fire and security systems to the definition of Section 179 property, will turn investments that you have rejected in the past into cash flow machines.

This is a whole new world of Real Estate Investing, and the quicker you learn the new rules, the quicker you build your new system.

I was an active Real Estate Investor and Attorney during the last major tax law overhaul, and it took about three years before we were in a position where it had morphed into its final form. I filed quite a few amended tax returns.

Then the Tax Court cases and the Federal District Court tax cases started coming down, and we made more adjustments.

So keep in mind, this is just the beginning. There will be changes.

But it looks great for Real Estate Investors, and most of that will probably not change.

MICHAEL LANTRIP

COPYRIGHT PAGE

Copyright 2018, 2019, 2020, 2021 Michael Lantrip.

All Rights Reserved.

Visit the author's website at:

www.MichaelLantrip.com.

Visit Amazon's Michael Lantrip Author Page at:

amazon.com/Michael-Lantrip/e/B01N2ZRGUY

Publisher: ANDERSON LOGAN, LLC

First Edition

ISBN 978-1945627064

This publication is designed to provide general information regarding the subject matter covered. Because each individual's legal, tax, and financial situation is different, specific advice should be tailored to those particular circumstances. For this reason, the reader is advised to consult with his or her own attorney, accountant, and/or other advisor regarding the reader's specific situation.

The Author has taken reasonable precautions in the preparation of this book and believes that the information presented in the book is accurate as of the date it was written. However, neither the Author nor the Publisher assumes any responsibility for any errors or omissions. The Author and the Publisher specifically disclaim any liability resulting from the use or application of the information contained in this book, and the information is not intended to serve as legal, tax, or other financial advice related to individual situations.

MICHAEL LANTRIP

DISCLAIMER

Although I am a lawyer, I am not your lawyer. I would be honored if I were, but I am not.

Reading this book does not create an attorney-client relationship between us. This book should not be used as a substitute for the advice of a competent attorney admitted or authorized to practice law in your jurisdiction.

CONTENTS

INTRODUCTION

CHAPTER 1. INDIVIDUAL TAX RATES

CHAPTER 2. CORPORATE TAX RATES

CHAPTER 3. CAPITAL GAINS

CHAPTER 4. PASS-THRU BUSINESS ENTITIES

CHAPTER 5. QUALIFIED BUSINESS INCOME

CHAPTER 6. INTEREST DEDUCTION LIMITATION

CHAPTER 7. MORTGAGE INTEREST LIMITS

CHAPTER 8. STATE & LOCAL TAX DEDUCTIONS

CHAPTER 9. SECTION 179 EXPENSING

CHAPTER 10. BONUS DEPRECIATION

CHAPTER 11. IRA PLAN CONTRIBUTIONS

CHAPTER 12. RETIREMENT PLAN LOANS

CHAPTER 13. ESTATE, GIFT, AND GST TAX

CHAPTER 14. ALTERNATIVE MINIMUM TAX

CHAPTER 15. KIDDIE TAX

CHAPTER 16. NET OPERATING LOSS

CHAPTER 17. EXCESS BUSINESS LOSSES

CHAPTER 18. CONCLUSION

MICHAEL LANTRIP

CHAPTER 1

INDIVIDUAL TAX RATES

I would make this more interesting if I could, but it is just one of those things you must know, because it affects every decision you will make.

WHAT IT IS

Each Taxpayer must pay some amount of taxes based on a computed number called Adjusted Gross Income, referred to as AGI.

Some Taxpayers are allowed to report their income, and take their deductions, together with another Taxpayer. This is determined by their Filing Status, or filing category.

There are four filing categories.

TCJA FOR REAL ESTATE INVESTORS

1.) Single (S).

2.) Married, Filing Jointly (MFJ).

3.) Married, Filing Separately (MFS).

4.) Head of Household (HH).

5.) Surviving Widows can qualify to file MFJ.

Each Taxpayer then falls into a Tax Bracket, from 10% to 37%, which refers to the taxable amount of the last dollar of marginal income.

The appropriate Tax Bracket for a Taxpayer will be determined by the Taxpayer's AGI.

SUMMARY OF THE NEW LAW

For individual Taxpayers, the highest marginal tax rate on ordinary income is reduced from 39.6% to 37%, and all of the other Tax Brackets are adjusted downward to result is a reduced tax liability on the same level of income.

NEW LAW EXPLAINED

The Tax Cuts And Jobs Act (TCJA) changes both the Tax Brackets and the cutoff amounts, as well as the Tax Rates.

I'll just do Single and MFJ since you are probably in one of these.

TAX BRACKETS

10% Tax Bracket

- Single: $0 – $9,525
- MFJ: $0 – $19,050

12% Tax Bracket

- Single: $9,526 – $38,700
- MFJ: $19,051 – $77,400

22% Tax Bracket

- Single: $38,701 – $82,500
- MFJ: $77,401 – $165,000

24% Tax Bracket

- Single: $82,501 – $157,500
- MFJ: $165,001 – $315,000

32% Tax Bracket

- Single: $157,501 – $200,000
- MFJ: $315,001 – $400,000

35% Tax Bracket

- Single: $200,001 – $500,000
- MFJ: $400,001 – $600,000

TCJA FOR REAL ESTATE INVESTORS

37% Tax Bracket

- Single: $500,001 and more
- MFJ: $600,001 and more

There are other income-related subjects, such as the Alternative Minimum Tax (AMT) which I will cover in Chapter 14, and Kiddie Tax in Chapter 15, and others that will be summarized as part of a related subject within a Chapter.

The Personal Exemption is eliminated, and the Standard Deduction is increased.

The new Standard Deduction is $12,000 for Singles, $24,000 for MFJs, and $18,000 for a Head of Household.

CHAPTER 2

CORPORATE TAX RATES

The Corporate Tax Rate has been reduced by 40%.

We have never had a reduction in the Corporate Tax Rate of this size in the history of the Tax Code, and it is having an enormous impact on the U.S. economy.

WHAT IT IS

The Corporation referred to in discussions of the Corporate Tax Rates is actually a "C Corporation."

This is a Corporation with stockholders. It accounts for its income at the corporate level and pays taxes at the corporate level. The money left over can then be retained by the Corporation for operating capital or any other purpose. But if it is distributed to the stockholders, who are actually the owners of the Corporation and therefore own the retained income in the same manner that they share ownership of other corporate assets, the retained income is characterized as "dividends" upon distribution, and treated as income to the stockholders, and therefore taxable, although the distributed funds represent the income of the Corporation and has already been taxed once.

There is one way in which an individual might be subject to the Corporate Tax Rate even though the individual is not a C Corporation.

If you form a Limited Liability Company (LLC), you will be treated as a "disregarded entity" and you will report your business activity on a Schedule C, or Schedule E, or Schedule F, and attach the Schedule to your Form 1040.

But "disregarded entity" is actually the "default" status, which will happen if you do nothing on your own to file with the IRS for a method in which you would like to be taxed for the LLC activities.

You are also allowed to file a form electing to have the LLC **taxed as a Corporation,** which means a C corporation, which you may not want.

The reason that people file the Election to be taxed as a Corporation is so that they can then file the Election to be treated as a Subchapter S Corporation (Sub S or S Corp). This causes the income and credits to "pass through" the Corporation without being taxed, and be reported on the returns of the owner or owners of the LLC.

But the Corporate Tax Rate that we are talking about is the tax rate for the standard C Corporation.

The top Corporate tax rate prior to the Tax Cuts And Jobs Act (TCJA) was 35%.

SUMMARY OF THE NEW LAW

To replace the graduated tax rate system for C Corporations which topped out at 35%, we now have a flat 21% tax rate for all C Corp income.

NEW LAW EXPLAINED

Unlike the new tax rates for individuals, which will expire in 2025 and revert back to the prior rates if no new legislation is passed, the new Corporate Tax Rate of 21% is permanent.

TCJA FOR REAL ESTATE INVESTORS

This permanency was necessary in order to provide some certainty for corporations because they operate in the "long-term world," and are usually operating with a 10-year or 20-year plan, often with losses expected in the early years, offset by profits after that.

Facing the possibility of a reversion to a 35% top tax rate would have killed a lot of the investment activity that will now happen under the TCJA.

And it is important to understand just how huge this corporate tax rate reduction really is.

You look at a reduction from 35% to 21% and you see a 14% reduction. Considering the large numbers we are dealing with for corporations, that is a pretty impressive amount of money that the businesses are now keeping, and either using it to grow the business, or to pay higher dividends to the stockholders, which will then result in an increase in the Corporation's stock prices.

But in reality, the reduction is really more than 14%.

The reduction is actually 40%.

The new rate of 21% is only 60% of the prior rate of 35%.

So, the amount of the reduction is really 40%.

I don't recall ever seeing any similar type of tax collected by the IRS reduced by 40%, and certainly not one of the major sources of revenue.

I don't think we can predict the magnitude of economic changes that are ahead due solely to this one tax change.

And the "other tax" that is seldom talked about because most of the discussion about it is about how to legally manipulate it, is the Alternative Minimum Tax (AMT).

It did not apply to corporations with average annual gross receipts of less than $7.5 million for the preceding three tax years, but for the rest, it was assessed at 20%.

The AMT was envisioned to prevent any Corporation from paying no taxes at all. It has never worked toward its intended purpose, and every attempt by the IRS to strengthen it has just made it more cumbersome and less effective.

Most small businesses are not subject to the AMT, but it is still significant to note that it has now been eliminated for corporations.

TCJA FOR REAL ESTATE INVESTORS

It is rare for the IRS to admit defeat like this, and the fact that they did offers some hope that they will also scrap the AMT for individual taxpayers, where it is an even bigger mess than the Corporate AMT was.

PLANNING OPPORTUNITIES

Since most real estate businesses are organized as either an LLC, Partnership, or a S Corp, if not a Sole Proprietor, the change will probably not concern you.

However, the new flat tax rate of 21% might be a reason to consider changing to a C Corp as the best business entity for operating real estate investments.

You still have the double taxation, but if you anticipate an extended period of time when the investment will not actually be making a profit, but providing other reasons for owning, the double taxation is not a problem.

C Corporations have always been a solid form of business structure, but maybe not for individuals who do not have the time to learn about them, or the process of creating one, or switching another existing entity over to a C Corp.

If you are thinking of revoking the Subchapter S status of your C Corporation, be careful. There are a number of issues to consider.

And two facts to keep in mind is that you must do it before March 15 of the tax year in which want the change to be effective, and once you change, you cannot elect Sub S status again for at least another five years.

But the business considerations are also quite serious.

For one Example, you probably have money in the account of your Sub S that is the result of business activities. It is income that has already been reported on the Form 1120S Income Tax Return for an S Corporation. It has already been reported to you and to the IRS on the Schedule K-1. You have already included it in your individual tax return as income and paid taxes on it.

It is what is called "after-tax income," but it is still being held in your Sub S account.

On your company books, it is tracked through an "accumulated adjustment account" (AAA) if it is tracked at all.

TCJA FOR REAL ESTATE INVESTORS

If you revoke your Sub S status with this money still where it is, it can impair your distribution of the money out of the C Corporation without treating it as a Dividend, and reporting it as such. It can be done, but it is complicated, and there are time constraints.

A better way to do it would be to issue Promissory Notes from the S Corp to the shareholders representing their proportional amount of the retained earnings, and then the money remains/becomes an asset of the C Corporation and the notes become liabilities, so it is a wash. And the notes will not be reportable income to the individual shareholders.

But this could become a problem if we are dealing with very large Promissory Notes, because the C Corporation will be paying interest on the notes in additional to the periodic principal payments.

The interest paid by the C Corporation will be deductible as a business expense, but it will be shielding income that would be taxed at 21%.

However, the interest on the notes will be taxable income to the shareholders (but not the principal), and the shareholders might be in a personal tax bracket much higher than 21%.

A better way to handle it might be for the Sub S to distribute all of the retained earnings to the shareholders prior to reversion to a C Corporation, then borrow the money back after the reversion, or issue a separate class of stock, with conversion privileges, for the shareholders to purchase.

Another problem with a S Corp to C Corp reversion is that there are also other assets which you might "trap" inside the C Corporation that could prove costly later on. You might have some high-dollar equipment, like a bulldozer, or a printing press, and you might at some point sell those at a profit, either because you bought at a good price, or they have gone up in value, or you have claimed most or all of the allowable depreciation.

Your Capital Gains will be taxed at the corporate level. Then when the proceeds are distributed to you, they will be taxed again at your individual level.

One way to avoid this problem is to distribute these assets to yourself while still a Sub S, and then lease them back to the corporation after reversion.

This will not only avoid the double taxation when they are sold (quadruple, if you consider state taxes), but this is a way that you can get money out of the corporation almost tax-free because you can still deduct depreciation from the lease payments before paying the taxes on them.

It also gives the corporation another expense to deduct from corporate income, even though the money is coming to you.

Most Sub S corporations that go through the process of considering whether to revert to C Corporation status probably will not do so.

And the benefits under the new TCJA for Pass-through Entities are almost as good as the 40% reduction in the corporate tax rate.

See Chapters 4 and 5 for more information.

CHAPTER 3

CAPITAL GAINS

The Tax Cuts And Jobs Act (TCJA) did not change the Capital Gains Tax amounts, they are still 0%, 15%, and 20%, but it messed with the individual Taxpayer tax brackets so that there is actually a change in the Capital Gains structure, at least the Short Term Capital Gains.

WHAT IT IS

One of the primary concerns for Real Estate Investors is Capital Gains.

Capital Gains are taxed according to the period of time the Taxpayer owned the capital asset before selling it.

If the asset is owned for one year or less, then the capital gains is characterized as Short-Term Capital Gains (STCG).

The tax applied to the STCG is the taxpayer's ordinary income tax bracket, from 10% to 37%.

Since the TCJA reduced the tax rates and tax brackets for individuals, it could be said that the new tax law does actually lower the Capital Gains tax rate.

But that would only be true for Short-Term Capital Gains.

The tax rate for Long-Term Capital Gains (LTCG) remains the same under the new law.

LTCG are gains on sold assets which were owned for at least a year and one day.

PRIOR LAW

Under the law in effect in 2017, the LTCG tax brackets were based on your ordinary income tax brackets.

It is important for you to read and understand this section because it will help you to understand my explanation later in this Chapter about how much of your LTCG is actually taxable, and what the appropriate tax rate is.

1.) If you were previously in the 10% or the 15% ordinary income tax bracket, your LTCG was subject to 0% tax (except that some of it wasn't, see below).

2.) If you were in the 25%, 28%, 33%, or 35% ordinary income tax bracket, your LTCG was subject to 15% tax (and maybe higher on some of it).

3.) If you were in the 39.6% ordinary income tax bracket, your LTCG was subject to 20% tax.

NEW LAW EXPLAINED

Under the new tax law, there are still only three tax rates for LTCG, and they are still 0%, 15%, and 20%.

However, even though the TCJA did not change the three tax rate amounts, the TCJA did change the Capital Gains tax structure by changing the brackets for each of the tax rates by establishing cutoff points, and indexing them for inflation.

The point at which the Capital Gains tax rate changes from 0% to a 15% tax rate is:

- $77,200 for Married Filing Jointly (MFJ) and Surviving Spouses,

- $38,600 for Married Filing Separately (MFS),

TCJA FOR REAL ESTATE INVESTORS

- $51,700 for Head of Household (HH),
- $2,600 for estates and trusts, and
- $38,600 for other unmarried individuals.

The point at which the 15% tax rate changes to a 20% tax rate is:

- $479,000 for MFJ and Surviving Spouses,
- $239,500 for MFS,
- $452,400 for HH,
- $12,700 for estates and trusts, and
- $425,800 for other unmarried individuals.

But the real question for Real Estate Investors, always, is how much tax you will pay, and that depends on the portion of your LTCG that is taxable, combined with the rate at which it is taxable.

We have to break it down and look at a number of different calculations to answer that question.

The LTCG tax rates are, in some ways, in the nature of the ordinary income tax rates, which are "marginal" tax rates, meaning when you reach a certain level, the next dollar is taxed at a higher rate.

If you are in the 0% LTCG tax bracket, it does not mean that all of your LTCG is non-taxable.

The IRS has two categories of income that we need to look at.

They actually have more, but we only need to look at two for this calculation.

The first income category is the old basic category of ordinary taxable income.

Ordinary income is defined as income other than Capital Gains and certain Dividends. It is wages, salaries, tips, commissions, bonuses, and any other type of income resulting from employment, as well as interest, ordinary dividends, and net income from a sole proprietorship or from a Pass-Through Entity (PTE) such as a Sub S, LLC, or Partnership.

The second income category is Capital Gains and certain Dividends.

The ordinary income category is what the LTCG tax brackets are based on.

The bracket amounts do not include your LTCG to determine which bracket you initially fall in.

In the world of the IRS, the LTCG is the "last" income that you received, even though, in reality, you might have sold the property on January 1.

TCJA FOR REAL ESTATE INVESTORS

Remember, we are playing by their rules, and we need to know what the rules are in order to use them to our advantage. Often they are not in sync with reality.

So, let's use an Example to see how this works.

You are a MFJ and your ordinary taxable income is $63,000. You sold a rent house after owning it for five years and claiming $10,000 in Depreciation. Your LTCG amount was $50,000.

Which LTCG tax bracket are you in, and how much is your tax?

Your first inclination is to say that your ordinary taxable income is $63,000 and that is less than the top (cutoff level) of the 0% tax bracket of $77,200 and does not put you into the next bracket, the 15% tax bracket, so the tax on your LTCG is 0%.

Your second inclination is to say that if you added your $50,000 LTCG to your $63,000 ordinary taxable income, the total would be $113,000 and put you into the 15% tax bracket, so all of your $50,000 LTCG would be taxable at 15%.

Both of those are incorrect.

It is true that you are in the 0% LTCG tax bracket because your ordinary taxable income is less than $77,200. And as long as you stay under $77,200 you will stay in the 0% bracket.

Now, here's the step in the process that is never discussed.

Your $63,000 of ordinary taxable income puts you in the 12% marginal income tax bracket for individuals.

That means that the first $19,050 of your ordinary taxable income will be taxed at 10%, and the remaining $43,950 will be taxed at 12%.

The total tax on your $63,000 of ordinary taxable income will be $1,905 + $5,274 = $7,179.

The $50,000 of LTCG will not bump you up into the 22% individual income tax bracket.

But you will have to add the $50,000 to the $63,000 to find out how much of the $50,000 is taxable as LTCG.

Of course, if you read my book, "How To Do A Section 1031 Like Kind Exchange," thank you, and you will recall that the first thing that we have to do with the $50,000 of LTCG is separate out the Depreciation portion because it will be treated separately.

The entire $50,000 is classified as LTCG, but the part of it that represents the Depreciation Recapture will be taxed at a different rate from the "pure" capital gains.

You claimed $10,000 in Depreciation and now must pay a tax on that amount.

The maximum amount of tax on Depreciation Recapture is 25%.

But that still leaves $40,000 of LTCG to account for here.

How is it taxed, 0% or 15%?

Well, both.

The portion of the LTCG that will carry your ordinary taxable income up to the top of the 0% tax bracket of $77,200 will be taxed at 0%.

This amount is $77,200 minus $63,000 = $14,200.

There will be no tax on the first $14,200 of your $40,000 LTCG.

The remaining amount that will be taxable at 15% will be $40,000 minus $14,200 = $25,800.

This is what I meant before when I said that the LTCG tax brackets are, in some ways, "marginal" like the ordinary income tax brackets.

Of course, if you had done something like taken a year off to finish a degree, or to travel, or to serve a prison sentence (just checking to see if you're paying attention), or some similar change in your lifestyle that caused you to have ordinary taxable income for this one year of $20,000, then your entire $50,000 of LTCG would have been non-taxable because the total of the two would be $70,000 and would still not move you out of the 0% LTCG tax bracket.

On the other hand, if your ordinary taxable income had been $83,000 instead of $63,000 all of your $50,000 LTCG would have been taxable, and at 15%.

As I have said often, knowledge of Depreciation and Capital Gains has accounted for as much as one-third of the profit that I have made from real estate investments.

I strongly encourage you to learn about these things, even if you don't find them fascinating, as I do. After all, it is how you make money, isn't it?

TCJA FOR REAL ESTATE INVESTORS

And finally, for matters pertaining to capital gains in the new tax law, the 25% tax on LTCG on the sale of small business stock is retained.

And the 28% tax on LTCG from the sale of collectibles is also retained. Collectibles are defined as works of art, rugs, antiques, gems, coins, stamps, and other items on the IRS list.

And, as I said, the Depreciation Recapture tax, often associated with Capital Gains transactions, is still taxed as a maximum of 25%.

CHAPTER 4

PASS-THROUGH BUSINESS ENTITIES

The biggest change in TCJA for Real Estate Investors is the way that Pass-Through Entities (PTEs) are now taxed, and it is also the most complicated.

Remember that the IRS defines Pass-Through Entities as "an entity that passes its income, losses, deductions, or credits to its owners, who might be partners, shareholders, beneficiaries, or investors."

Previously, the total income and credits of your LLC, Partnership, or Sub S Corp were just passed through to you, placed on your personal tax return, and taxed at your personal income level.

TCJA FOR REAL ESTATE INVESTORS

Now, we must deconstruct our activities and look at three separate elements.

- Is our business a Pass-Through Entity (PTE)?
- Is the PTE engaged in a Qualified Trade or Business (QTB)?
- How much is the Qualified Business Income (QBI) 20% Exclusion?

In this Chapter we will look at the PTE and answer the QTB question, and then cover QBI exclusion amount in the next Chapter.

Don't worry, you'll get used to these terms soon, and it will greatly enhance your understanding of what you read everywhere else about the new law.

Your choice of business entity is probably the most important decision you will ever make regarding your real estate investing career.

The choice will affect:

- the acquisition and disposition of real property,
- the construction of improvements on the property,
- the financing of the acquisition and improvements,

- the rental activities of the property,

- the business management of the investment, and

- the transfer of ownership of the property.

If you are currently an active Real Estate Investor, you need to look at the question of whether you should continue to operate in the same manner, in light of the new tax law.

If you are about to purchase your first, or next, investment property, you need to make the choice of the best business entity for the endeavor.

Let's look at the various business entity choices.

1.) Sole Proprietorship. You do not have any type of legal entity structure and you are operating just as an individual. You report your income and expenses on Schedule C or Schedule E and attach it to your Form 1040 Individual Income Tax Return. You have no limit on your personal liability from things that happen in your business operations.

2.) Partnership. This is when the business operation is owned by more than one individual. Income and expenses are allocated according to percentage ownership. Liability is "joint and several" which means that each person is totally responsible for any adverse claim arising from business operations, and in some cases from the behavior of the other partner. Income and expenses can be reported on Form 1065 Partnership Return of Income, and then profit/loss and credits distributed to the partners through the use of a Schedule K-1 to be reported on their individual tax returns, or, instead of doing a Form 1065 Return, the income and expenses of the operation can be divided and allocated according to percentage ownership and each partner can report that portion on Schedule C. Partnerships may or may not have a written Partnership Agreement, and can be either a General Partnership or a Limited Partnership. An LLC with more than one member will be taxed as a General Partnership as the default classification.

    3.) Limited Liability Company (LLC). This affords the individual the limit on personal liability that is available from a corporation, but without as much corporate formality. The LLC can elect to be treated for tax purposes as a Partnership or as a Corporation. If choosing to be taxed as a Corporation, the LLC can then elect Subchapter S status, and have the income pass through to the individual owners.

4.) **Single Member Limited Liability Company (SMLLC).** If the LLC has only one owner, that owner will be treated as a "disregarded entity" for tax purposes by the IRS as the default classification, and the owner can report income and expenses on Schedule C or Schedule E, the same as being a sole proprietor. But the owner can elect to be treated as a Corporation by filing the required election form. Then the owner can elect Subchapter S status and have the income pass through to be taxed at the individual level.

5.) **C Corporation (C Corp).** This is the most common type of business, and the one used by most public companies. The corporation issues stock which represents ownership of the company. The stockholders elect a Board of Directors to manage the company. The Board of Directors chooses company officers such as President, Vice President, Secretary, and Treasurer to run the company. The income of the company is reported at the company level and taxes are paid at the company level on the income by filing Form 1120 Corporate Tax Return. The company owns the profits. Company profits may or may not be distributed to the shareholders after each tax year, or at any time, as dividends. If dividends are paid, the shareholder then must report the dividends as income, and pay taxes, although the corporation has already been taxed on the same income, hence the term "double taxation" which is usually applied to C Corps.

6.) Professional Service Corporation (P.C.). This is a category for corporations and is reserved for use by some professionals such as doctors, architects, and attorneys. It differs from the regular corporation because it does not provide a shield against liability. It is considered to be in the public interest that these individuals be held liable for all of their conduct and activities, and should not be allowed to shield themselves from that liability through incorporation, like other citizens are allowed to do, such as car salesmen, wrecker services, driveway repairmen, carpenters and plumbers, and stock brokers.

7.) S Corporation (S Corp). An S Corp is not really another type of corporation. It is actually a C Corp which has filed an election to be treated as a Subchapter S Corporation, and have the income, losses, deductions and credits flow through to the shareholders for taxation at the individual level. The S Corp actually files a corporate tax return just like a C Corp, but uses the Form 1120S, which is an 1120 that is adjusted for use by an S Corp. Prior to the creation of the LLC laws, the S Corp was the primary method of avoiding the double taxation of the corporate form, but still allow the individual to enjoy the limit against liability.

All of these entities except the C Corp, and the P.C. are PTEs and will be affected by the new tax law by being able to exclude up to 20% of their income from taxation.

To repeat, business income that passes through a PTE to an individual, and Sole Proprietorship income, will be taxed at the individual's tax rate, AFTER EXCLUDING UP TO 20% OF THE INCOME.

I will refer to the 20% as an "exclusion" instead of a "deduction" because it is an exclusion.

The exclusion does not apply to interest, dividend, or capital gains income, just to business income.

It sounds like a great deal, until you actually read the rule.

You might want to turn away at this point, this is pretty ugly.

"The deduction is the sum of the lesser of the Combined Qualified Business Income, or 20% of the excess of the taxable income divided by the sum of any net capital gain, added to the lesser of 20% of the aggregate amount of the qualified cooperative dividends of the taxpayer, or the taxable income reduced by the net capital gain."

And, the "Combined Qualified Business Income" referred to in the above explanation is defined as "the lesser of 20% of the qualified business income with respect to the qualified trade or business, or the greater of 50% of the W-2 wages with respect to the qualified trade or business, or the sum of 25% of the W-2 wages with respect to the qualified trade or business, plus 2.5% of the unadjusted basis immediately after acquisition of all qualified property."

Did you get that?

Have you ever read such gibberish?

This new rule is a pig's breakfast, because the IRS always writes everything starting with the backend, or the exceptions.

But we can figure it out, and we might even understand it when we are finished.

The first thing that we need to understand is that there has been a change in terminology that has confused the explanation.

The rule talks about "Qualified Business Income" and you would naturally think that the term means "business income" that somehow needs to be "qualified," as in "qualified business income."

It does not mean that.

The PTEs that I told you about above that now qualify for the exclusion of 20% of their income from taxation, are now being referred to as a "Qualified Business" instead of being engaged in a "Qualified Trade or Business (QTB)."

In other words, they are "businesses" that "qualify" for the 20% income exclusion.

So, "Qualified Business Income" just means the income from a Pass-Through Entity (PTE), now called a "Qualified Business."

Let's move on to the next Chapter and find out how to calculate this income.

CHAPTER 5

QUALIFIED BUSINESS INCOME

"Qualified Business Income" (QBI) is the income from a "qualified trade or business."

A "qualified trade or business," as explained in the prior Chapter, is a Pass-Through Entity (PTE).

A Pass-Through Entity (PTE) is "an entity that passes its income, losses, deductions, or credits to its owners, who might be partners, shareholders, beneficiaries, or investors."

There are certain "service trades or businesses" which do not qualify as a "qualified trade or business," and we won't go into them here, because the renting of real property and real estate development both meet the definition of "qualified trade or business."

And QBI does not include interest, dividends, or capital gains.

QBI only includes the income from the operation of the qualified business.

The amount of the exclusion from taxation is 20% of the QBI.

If your total taxable income from all sources is $50,000, and your QBI is $40,000, you can exclude $8,000 from taxation, which is 20% of the $40,000 QBI.

Nice and simple so far.

But this is where it starts getting complicated (and it never stops).

You might not be able to take the entire 20%, because there are limitations and exclusions.

The limitations and exclusions start with the Threshold Amount.

This is the amount that you must be <u>under</u> in order to qualify.

TCJA FOR REAL ESTATE INVESTORS

The Threshold Amount is $157,500 for individual taxpayers, and it is $315,000 for married taxpayers filing jointly.

This is not your QBI, this is your total taxable income.

If your total taxable income is below the Threshold Amount, your QBI exclusion amount is simply 20% of the QBI for each of your qualified businesses. QBI is determined on a "per business," not a "per taxpayer," basis.

You don't have to deal with the complications contained in the remainder of the rule. You're finished.

But if your taxable income is above the Threshold Amount, you are still dealing with the 20% of QBI situation, but there is a second exclusion that you must also calculate.

Then you are only entitled to take the smaller of the two exclusions, the 20% exclusion or the new exclusion amount.

Your new exclusion is called the "wage and capital limit."

The "wage and capital limit" is the greater of:

1.) 50% of W-2 wages with respect to your trade or business, or

2.) the sum of 25% of these W-2 wages, plus 2.5% of the unadjusted basis, immediately after acquisition, of all qualified property.

"Qualified property" is tangible property subject to depreciation and available for use in your business at the end of the tax year, and used in the production of the QBI.

Now, let's do an Example.

- You are Married, Filing Jointly (MFJ) and your total taxable income is $350,000.

- Your QBI is $75,000.

- Your W-2 wages are $20,000.

- Your qualified property is $160,000.

Your 20% exclusion of the $75,000 QBI would be $15,000 if you were not over the Threshold Amount. But you are. Your $350,000 taxable income puts you $35,000 over the $315,000 Threshold Amount for MFJ.

So, you must calculate the two factors in your new second exclusion amount.

TCJA FOR REAL ESTATE INVESTORS

For the first one, 50% of your W-2 wages of $20,000 is $10,000.

For the second one, 25% of your W-2 wages ($5,000) added to 2.5% of your qualified property of $160,000 ($4,000) is $9,000.

Your new exclusion amount is $10,000 because that is the greater of the two amounts that you just calculated.

And since the new exclusion amount of $10,000 is lower than the 20% exclusion amount of $15,000, you must now claim the new lower exclusion amount of $10,000.

But you don't get the entire amount like you would if your total taxable income was just $1 over the Threshold Amount, instead of $35,000 over.

There is a Phase Out Period for the $100,000 over the Threshold Amount. During this period, the exclusion amount is prorated.

The Phase Out Period for MFJ taxpayers starts at $315,000 and goes up to $415,000, at which point the exclusion disappears altogether.

To find out where you are, we take your total taxable income of $350,000 and subtract $315,000, the Threshold Amount, and get $35,000. This is where you are on that $100,000 Phase Out line.

Then we divide $35,000 by the $100,000 and we get 35%.

Then we multiply 35% times the $10,000 exclusion that we calculated, and we get the amount of the exclusion that we are not entitled to because of the level of total taxable income being $350,000.

That means that we are still entitled to 65% of the $10,000.

And 65% of the $10,000 exclusion is $6,500.

This is the amount of our exclusion at this total income level and with this set of factors.

I hope this helps you understand this mess.

Now remember that we still have the "technical corrections" that will be coming out during the year to explain or expand on the rule, and eventually we will have the Treasury Regulations that will also explain the rule, using Examples.

CHAPTER 6

INTEREST DEDUCTION LIMITATION

This rule is actually a rewrite of Section 163(j) of the Internal Revenue Code.

It places a 30% limit on the amount of interest charges that you then deduct as a business expense.

The rule only applies to businesses with average annual receipts for the last three years of at least $25 million, so the limitation might not apply to you.

But you should still learn about it because it is part of your knowledge of the real estate business, and your knowledge of business in general.

The rule applies to both C Corporations and Pass-Through Entities (PTEs), as well as Sole Proprietorships.

Remember that the IRS defines PTEs as "an entity that passes its income, losses, deductions, or credits to its owners, who might be partners, shareholders, beneficiaries, or investors."

In essence, the 30% limitation is applied to "net" business interest expenses. In other words, the excess of your business interest expense over the interest income portion of your business income. But it is not explained that way.

The new rule limits the deduction for "business interest" to the sum of the Taxpayer's "business interest income" plus 30% of the Taxpayer's "adjusted taxable income" (ATI).

ATI is defined in general terms as your earnings before interest, taxes, depreciation, and amortization, commonly referred to as EBITDA.

More specifically, ATI is defined as taxable income calculated without regard to:

- any item of income, gain, deduction or loss that cannot be allocated to the business,

- business interest or business interest income,

TCJA FOR REAL ESTATE INVESTORS

- available NOL deductions,
- the new 20% QBI deduction, or
- any depreciation, amortization, or depletion deductions.

"Business interest" is defined as any interest paid or accrued on indebtedness that is "properly allocable to a trade or business."

I don't know why you would be trying to deduct interest expense that was not "properly allocable to a trade or business," but the Internal Revenue Code is a vast and mysterious world, and there is probably some way to do it.

However, after you decide what your limitation is, the portion of the interest amount that does not fall under the 30% limitation can be carried forward indefinitely and treated as business interest paid or accrued in future tax years until it is all used.

The rule also allows real property businesses, and businesses engaged in farming, to opt out of the new 30% limitation on business interest deductions.

Real Estate Businesses that qualify are:

- Real property development or redevelopment,
- Construction or reconstruction,

- Property acquisition,
- Rental and operation,
- Management or leasing, and
- Brokerage.

But in opting out, the Taxpayer gives up the use of the depreciation of residential rental property over a 27.5-year period and commercial property for 39 years, available under the Modified Accelerated Cost Recovery System, referred to as MACRS, and must use the Alternative Depreciation System (ADS) depreciation period.

The alternative period is 30 years and 40 years respectively, and the alternative depreciation period increases the newly-created category period of 15 years for Qualified Improvement Property to 20 years.

One very important item to keep in mind if you are considering opting out of the MACRS system is that you will not be allowed to take "bonus depreciation," the immediate expensing of certain assets.

This is critical for Real Estate Investors because the new rules regarding Bonus Depreciation are expected to cover "qualified improvement property."

TCJA FOR REAL ESTATE INVESTORS

I say "expected to" because the hastily-written law was not clear on the matter, and this will probably be dealt with along with the other "technical corrections" that the TCJA is expected to generate.

Also, there is considerable uncertainty as to how you actually accomplish the change from MACRS to ADS if you are already in the middle of depreciating a bunch of assets under the MACRS. Do you start over, or do you just add the additional years onto the period you are already using?

And remember that the election to opt out is permanent, and is irrevocable.

All in all, the interest deduction limitation will probably not affect you and your business activities, but if it does, be cautious about doing anything that will change what you were doing before.

Spend time with a tax professional, and get his report in writing and keep it in your files if you do make any changes.

CHAPTER 7

MORTGAGE INTEREST DEDUCTION LIMITS

Individuals who are homeowners are usually paying one or more of the following types of interest which could be deductible:

- on a mortgage created to acquire the primary residence,

- on a home equity loan on the primary residence, or

- on a home equity loan on a vacation home.

The loan interest could be on their primary residence and one other residence that either is not rented out at all, such as a vacation home, or is rented but used by the taxpayer for the minimum number of days to qualify.

The interest on all of these debts was previously deductible on Schedule A as an Itemized Deduction, with a limit of $1M on the mortgage amount on the primary residence.

Now, for property purchased after December 31, 2017, the deduction for mortgage interest related to the acquisition of property is limited to underlying indebtedness of $750,000. For married taxpayers filing separately, the amount is $375,000.

Refinance debt is treated the same as acquisition debt if it does not exceed the principal balance of the acquisition debt just prior to the refinance, and meets the $750,000/375,000 limit.

Home Equity debt is different from a refinance.

The debt is secured by the principal residence, and under the old tax law the interest was deductible even if the proceeds were used for personal expenses.

However, there was a limit of $100,000 of debt for everyone else, and $50,000 for Married Filing Separate (MFS).

Also, the debt could not be more than the actual Equity in the residence.

If these limits were exceeded, the interest on the extra amount of debt was treated as personal, and not deductible.

Under the Tax Cuts and Jobs Act, the interest deduction for Equity debt is eliminated.

Of course, if funds from a refinance, or funds from an Equity loan, are used to repair or substantially improve the taxpayer's primary residence or one other residence, the interest on those funds is deductible.

Also, if the funds are used for a business or to purchase or improve rental property or other investment property, then the interest on those loan payments is deductible as a business expense on Schedule C or Schedule E, or the entity's tax return if the entity is required to file one, but not as an Itemized Deduction on Schedule A, Form 1040.

And the amount is not subject to any limitation amount.

However, you must be very careful to document everything and keep good records.

And, of course, if you are a Real Estate Investor with rental property and you get an equity loan secured by the rental property, that interest is also deductible, and for the same reason. The interest is a business expense of operating the income-producing investment.

And the $750,000/$375,000 limitation on deductible mortgage interest does not apply to Real Estate Investors who take out a mortgage on an investment property. That is a business loan, and the interest on a business loan is always a deductible expense.

To repeat, interest is a deductible expense in the operation of an investment property.

But interest on a loan where you use the proceeds for personal expenses is considered personal interest, and is not deductible regardless of the nature of the property that is securing that loan.

And, of course, all business interest deduction is now limited by the new law, as described here in Chapter 6.

CHAPTER 8

STATE AND LOCAL TAX DEDUCTIONS

WHAT IT IS

State and Local income taxes which you paid this year, covering the taxes on the income for the prior year, are still deductible. But see below. The same rules apply in states which have no income tax but that allow deduction of a computed amount of Sales Tax, as well as states that allow you to choose whether to deduct Sales Tax instead of State and Local income taxes.

You deduct these taxes on your Schedule A Itemized Deductions form which you attach to your Form 1040 Individual Income Tax Return.

TCJA FOR REAL ESTATE INVESTORS

Whether or not you get any benefit from the deduction of your State and Local taxes will depend on whether the total amount of all of the itemized deductions on your Schedule A exceeds the Standard Deduction which you are allowed to use instead of itemizing your deductions.

Property Taxes which you paid this year to satisfy a tax liability covering this year, or a prior years delinquency, might also still be deductible, and will also be deducted on Schedule A in the same manner as the State and Local income taxes described above.

NEW TAX LAW

Under the new TCJA, your deduction for the combined total of State and Local taxes, plus Property Taxes, is limited to $5,000 if you are single, and $10,000 if you are married, filing jointly.

But if you are a Real Estate Investor, and the Property Taxes you paid were Property Taxes for an investment rental property, then the full amount of the taxes are deductible as an expense on your Schedule C or Schedule E, wherever you report the income and expenses of your rental activities.

PLANNING OPPORTUNITIES

There is almost no way to massage the numbers in this area.

It is just one of the negatives in the new TCJA.

But one of the big positives in the new tax law is that the amount you are allowed in Standard Itemized Deductions if you do not itemize has been increased from $12,000 to $24,000 for Married Filing Jointly taxpayers.

It will relieve the burden for some.

CHAPTER 9

SECTION 179 EXPENSING

Section 179 has now been revised so that real estate investing activities are now included in the immediate expensing provisions.

If you cannot use the new 100% Bonus Depreciation provision, Section 179 can provide you similar benefits.

The new version of Section 179 will allow some Taxpayers to deduct the entire cost of qualifying depreciable property in the first year that it is placed in service, and for the first time it includes used property as well a new property.

PRIOR LAW

Property included was most depreciable personal property as well as "off the shelf" computer software.

But as for buildings or other land improvements, the only ones that qualified were restaurant buildings and certain building improvements to leased space, retail space, or restaurant space (leasehold improvements).

Prior law limited the Section 179 depreciation deduction to $510,000 for the tax year 2017.

NEW LAW

For qualifying property placed in service beginning in 2018, the maximum Section 179 deduction is increased to $1 million, and will be indexed for inflation in years after that.

The categories of restaurant buildings and certain building improvements to leased space, retail space, or restaurant space are eliminated and replaced with a much broader category called "qualified improvement property," referred to as QIP.

The new law has also changed the definition of qualified real property eligible for the Section 179 deduction to include the following improvements to nonresidential real estate:

1.) roofs,

2.) HVAC equipment,

3.) fire protection and alarm systems, and

4.) security systems.

The only requirement is that these roofs and other properties not relate to residential buildings.

However, some items such as refrigerators and stoves used in connection with residential buildings are eligible for Section 179 treatment.

Also, TCJA expands the definition of Section 179 property to include certain depreciable tangible property used predominantly to furnish lodging, or in connection with furnishing lodging, and this should include furniture and beds used in hotels and apartment buildings.

The QIP, in addition to no longer qualifying for Bonus Depreciation, and becoming newly eligible as Section 179 property, now has a 15-year depreciation period rather than a 39-year period that usually applies to non-residential buildings.

Another bonus for Real Estate Investors is that computers and related equipment are no longer classified as the dreaded "listed property" which contained strange rules and required jumping through hoops to get the benefit of depreciation.

And the computer and related equipment use is no longer limited to a business office or home office, and they don't have to pass the 50% qualified business use test.

PLANNING OPPORTUNITIES

This would be a risky area in which to make concrete changes that you will have to live with in the future.

We have not yet seen all of the technical corrections to the law, and that might take over a year. These changes could change the current interpretation of the rules.

We also have not seen the Treasury Regulations which will explain the meaning of the law and how it should be applied.

Caution should be the byword for you until you know for sure what the future holds in the areas of importance to you.

CHAPTER 10

BONUS DEPRECIATION

The largest benefit in the Tax Cuts and Jobs Act might be the 20% exclusion from taxable income for PTEs, but the 100% Bonus Depreciation Deduction is certainly the second largest.

The new law broadens the definition of property that qualifies for Bonus Depreciation, and also increases the maximum amounts of annual depreciation available.

It has the effect of lowering your cost of acquiring capital assets.

PRIOR LAW

Except for buildings and some building improvements, Taxpayers were able to deduct 50% of the cost of new tangible property and most new computer software in the year that it was purchased and placed in service.

The remaining Basis in the asset had to be depreciated over the assigned life, but starting in that first year.

And, used assets did not qualify.

A fact that received very little attention was that the 50% of Bonus Depreciation was scheduled to be reduced to 40% in the years 2018 and 2019, and then reduced to 0%.

NEW LAW

Perhaps the greatest change in the Bonus Depreciation rule is not the increase from 50% to 100%, but the fact that the property eligible for the new rate can be used property.

Being able to deduct the entire cost of used capital assets with bonus depreciation instead of having to spread it out over the asset life will spur all types of real estate investments.

TCJA FOR REAL ESTATE INVESTORS

The new rule covers purchased business assets such as furniture, fixtures, appliances, equipment, computers, and similar items, with useful lives of less than 20 years, and is available for the first year that the item is placed in service.

The recovery period for real estate assets exceeds 20 years and thus real estate assets do not qualify for expensing, but other associated tangible personal property may qualify.

However, the new law has eliminated Bonus Depreciation on a new category of property that it calls "qualified improvement property," referred to as QIP.

QIP is certain improvements to buildings that are not residential rental buildings. This category formerly included "leasehold improvements."

QIP is now eligible to be treated as Section 179 property and also has a new 15-year depreciable life instead of the 39 years that generally applies to non-residential buildings.

It is still possible that QIP will be eligible for Bonus Depreciation, even though it was not specifically provided for in the language of the TCJA.

Other comments in the early drafting documents indicate that it was the intention of the drafters that QIP be included, and this is shown by the fact that QIP depreciation was changed from 39 years to 15 years, thereby bringing it into the definition of "tangible personal property with a recovery period of 20 years or less," which is the definition of property eligible for Bonus Depreciation.

The rule covers the purchase of machinery, equipment, office furniture, computer systems, software, and even vehicles.

The prior law on vehicle depreciation was the one referred to as the "luxury automobile depreciation limitation" although it was not about luxury automobiles at all.

IRC Section 280F(a) covered all "passenger automobiles."

These are defined as vehicles that weigh up to 6,000 pounds.

And the category covers cars, vans, and trucks, including SUVs.

It applied only to new vehicles.

The new law significantly increases the maximum amount of annual depreciation allowed on qualifying vehicles.

TCJA FOR REAL ESTATE INVESTORS

But there are special rules applied to vehicles.

In addition to the requirement that the vehicle must be used over 50% for business, the maximum annual allowable depreciation deductions under the new TCJA are:

- $10,000 in the first year,
- $16,000 in the second year,
- $9,600 in the third year, and
- $5,760 in the fourth year and each successive year.

And remember that the first year amount of up to $10,000 is in addition to a Section 179 deduction of up to $8,000. So the first year total could potentially by $18,000.

PLANNING OPPORTUNITIES

The 100% Bonus Depreciation will only last through 2022, so it is best to plan ahead.

After 2022, the amount will be decreased to:

- 80% in 2023,
- 60% in 2024,

- 40% in 2025,
- 20% in 2026, and
- 0% in 2027 and thereafter.

CHAPTER 11

RETIREMENT PLAN AND IRA CONTRIBUTIONS

There are two types of individual retirement accounts (IRAs).

One is the traditional IRA, referred to simply as an "IRA," where <u>pre-tax</u> income is contributed to the account, and that income is excluded from taxation for the tax year, and the increases to the account in future years are not taxable until the money in the account is withdrawn, at which time the withdrawals are taxable at the Taxpayer's personal tax rate at that time.

The other type of IRA is the "Roth IRA," where <u>after-tax</u> income is contributed to the account, and the increases to the principal are exempt from taxation until they are withdrawn. The principal contributed is not taxable when withdrawn because it was after-tax money when put into the account.

One of the features associated with both the IRA and the Roth IRA is that before the due date of the taxpayer's tax return for the year, the taxpayer is allowed to "convert" a contribution made to one of the accounts as a contribution made to the other account.

The conversion is accomplished by way of a trustee-to-trustee transfer.

It effectively reverses the contribution from a traditional IRA to a Roth IRA, or from a Roth IRA to a traditional IRA.

The date of the contribution to the first account is used as the date of the contribution to the second account, the one to which it was transferred.

The amount transferred must be accompanied by any net income allocable to the contribution, and it applies only to the extent that no deduction was allowed for the contribution to the original account.

The deadline for making the conversion includes the time period of any extensions of time to file the taxpayer's return.

Conversions are more than just a matter of the Taxpayer having a change of mind. There is a strategy in doing so. For Example, the IRA owner could decide to re-characterize Roth IRA conversion contributions because the Roth IRA assets have declined in value after the conversion.

The eventual tax liability will be based on the value of the IRA assets at the time of the conversion. So, if the value of the assets is subject to large ups and downs during the year, the conversion and timing can be critical.

Under the Tax Cuts And Jobs Act, re-characterization of Roth IRA conversions are no longer permitted.

If a contribution to a regular IRA has been converted to a Roth IRA, it can no longer be converted back into a contribution to a regular IRA.

The first conversion from a regular IRA into a Roth IRA cannot be undone, or "re-characterized."

The rule that allow the contribution of one type of account to be re-characterized as a contribution to the other type of account no longer includes a converted contribution to a Roth IRA.

However, the law still permits conversion of a contribution to a Roth IRA for a tax year to be converted to a traditional IRA before the due date, including extensions, of the taxpayer's income tax return for that year, and vice versa.

CHAPTER 12

RETIREMENT PLAN LOANS

Some employees take part in their employer's retirement plan, and the plan might be one that permits the employee to borrow from the retirement plan without having the proceeds of the loan be considered taxable as a distribution from the plan.

Loans are not allowed from a traditional IRA, SIMPLE IRA, or a SEP. Doing so will invalidate the entire program and cause all of the balance in the account to be included in the account owner's income.

In order to be a plan that allows loans to employees, the employer's retirement plan must be a "Qualified Plan."

That means that it must be either:

- a qualified plan that meets IRS requirements, or

- an annuity plan that meets IRS requirements, or

- a government plan.

The loan must be in writing and meet the other requirements of a regular commercial loan, and must also meet other specific requirements.

1.) The loan must be repaid within five years, except when the loan proceeds are used to purchase the taxpayer's principal residence. This exception does not include refinancing of the principal residence. If the loan period is five years or less and there is a balance due at the end of the five-year period, the balance is paid from the plan participant's plan balance, and is considered a "deemed distribution." This means that it is taxable, and will probably also be subject to the 10% penalty for an early distribution if the taxpayer has not reached the required age.

2.) All of the payments over the life of the loan must be approximately equal. Balloon payments are not allowed. Payments may be suspended for up to one year for employees taking a leave of absence from the job, and for employees while they are serving in the military on active duty. However, the payments must be made up when the employee returns, and the term of the loan still cannot exceed the original limit. Payments do not have to be made monthly, but must be at least quarterly.

3.) The amount of the loan can only be up to one-half (1/2) of the present value of the plan participant's vested interest in the plan, or $50,000, whichever is less.

If the borrower defaults in making loan payments, the balance of the loan will be paid from the participant's account, and the amount of the payment will be reported to the IRS as an Early Distribution, and will be subject to the 10% Penalty as well as income tax.

A "deemed distribution" such as this is not qualified for rollover to another eligible retirement plan, as an "actual distribution" might be under different circumstances.

An "actual distribution" occurs if an employee quits or is laid off and the loan is automatically accelerated and the employee does not pay. The loan balance is paid from the employee's retirement account balance, and this is considered an "actual distribution."

The distinction between a "deemed distribution" and an "actual distribution" is critical because a loan offset is treated as an actual distribution from the retirement plan to the plan participant, and an actual distribution qualifies to be "rolled over" tax-free to another eligible retirement plan within 60 days, because of the termination of employment.

A "deemed distribution" cannot be rolled over.

Under the Tax Cuts And Jobs Act, the time allowed for a tax-free rollover of a qualified plan loan offset amount to be contributed to an eligible retirement plan is extended beyond the 60-day limit.

There has long been a concern that the 60-day limit is unfairly harsh for a taxpayer who has just become unemployed, and who has had to default on a loan because the entire principal balance became due.

The new time limit is the due date, including extensions, of the taxpayer's federal income tax return covering the tax year in which the plan loan offset occurred.

The amount that must be contributed to a new retirement plan is the amount that was taken from the previous plan balance to pay off the loan.

CHAPTER 13

ESTATE, GIFT AND GST TAX

The basic exclusion amount for gift tax and federal estate tax, and the exemption amount for the generation-skipping transfer (GST) tax has been doubled from $5M to $10M, and with the inflation adjustment for transfer taxes in effect for each year since 2011, the $10M is expected to actually be $11.2M for 2018.

This amounts to a $22.4M exemption for the estate of a married couple.

The Estate Tax and Gift Tax rates are combined in one table for the sake of uniformity.

The Unified Estate and Gift Tax rate starts at 18% on the first $10,000 and goes up to 40% on transfers over $1M.

There is a 100% Marital Deduction for property transferred to a spouse. That property will be taxed when the spouse dies if it is still in the estate.

The term "transfer taxes" refers to all three: the gift tax, the federal estate tax, and the GST tax.

The gift tax is a tax on the taxpayer's asset transfers during his or her lifetime.

The federal estate tax refers to the tax on certain transfers at death.

And the GST tax is the tax on transfers either directly or through a trust or similar arrangement to a recipient other than one in the next generation.

We will look at each in turn.

GIFT TAX

A gift tax is imposed on the transfer of property by gift during a tax year by any taxpayer.

The taxpayer's gift tax amount is determined by subtracting the annual gift tax exclusion, and allowable deductions, from the total gifting.

In order to determine the Gift Tax liability:

1.) Use the gift and estate tax tables to calculate a tentative tax for the combined current year and prior years,

TCJA FOR REAL ESTATE INVESTORS

2.) Calculate the tentative tax on prior year gifts,

3.) Subtract the tentative tax on all prior year gifts from the tentative tax on the combined current and prior years, to determine the portion of the total amount attributable to the current year, and

4.) Subtract the amount of unified credit not used by prior year gifts.

The value of the gifted property is considered to be the Fair Market Value (FMV) of the property at the time the gift is made.

If you intend to gift property that you believe is actually worth less than what other similar property is bought and sold for (the FMV value) then you can get an appraisal done by a reputable licensed Appraiser and hold it in case your stated value is ever questioned by the IRS.

In situations where you sell property for less than the FMV, you will be considered by the IRS to have made a gift of the difference to the Buyer. The IRS will use the FMV, not the sales price.

You are permitted to gift up to $15,000 to an individual each year without incurring a Gift Tax. And you can make as many of these gifts to as many people as you wish during the tax year.

Married couples can gift back and forth to each other and not be subject to the Gift Tax.

Also, the $15,000 annual exclusion is available to each spouse for gifts to other individuals.

And if one spouse agrees, the other spouse can use both exclusions together, and gift up to $30,000 to any number of singular recipients without triggering the Gift Tax.

ESTATE TAX

When a taxpayer dies, there is a tax levied on the estate of the deceased, called an Estate Tax.

The estate, also called the Taxable Estate, consists of the property of the deceased passing to other ownership due to the death.

It does not include all of the assets of the deceased, just the gross estate less certain allowable deductions, including a marital deduction for certain bequests to the surviving spouse, as well as certain charitable bequests.

The value of the property of the estate is determined to be the Fair Market Value (FMV) of the property on the date of death (DOD), or in some circumstances, six months after the DOD.

The estate also includes property not described above, which is added back. These are:

1.) Certain gifts made within the three years prior to the DOD.

2.) Certain transfers in which the deceased retained a Life Estate.

3.) Certain transfers which became effective on the DOD.

4.) Revocable transfers.

Also, a person might have something called a "power of appointment." This means that he or she has the right to designate who will become the owner of certain property on the DOD. If so, this property is also included in the estate.

GST TAX

In addition to the Gift Tax and Estate Tax, which are usually considered to be linked, there is a third tax on transfers that is imposed separately.

It is the generation-skipping transfer (GST) tax, referred to as the GST Tax.

It applies to transfers that go, either directly or in trust, to a recipient more than one generation below the individual doing the transfer.

In other words, it "skips" a generation, the generation below the deceased. Hence, the name, "generation-skipping transfer."

The tax is imposed on GSTs that are in excess of the GST exemption amount, which is equal to the Estate Tax exemption amount in effect for the same time period.

But it is the same exemption, not two, and the Executor or Administrator of the estate allocates the available amount between the tax liabilities.

The tax imposed on a GST is the highest estate tax rate of 40% multiplied by something called the "exclusion ratio," which is the amount of generation-skipping transfer tax exemption allocated to the skip property, in relation to the transferred property.

But the most important fact for Real Estate Investors is that the rule for the step-up in basis was retained.

If you pass real property to your heirs at death through inheritance, their basis in the property is raised to the fair market value of the property at the time of death.

This means that if they sell the property within a reasonable amount of time, usually about six months, then their basis in the property will be presumed to be the amount of the sales price.

Not only will they owe no Capital Gains tax on the transaction, but if you acquired the property through a Section 1031 Like Kind Exchange, or a series of Section 1031 Exchanges, and deferred all of the past Capital Gains taxes and Depreciation Recapture taxes, your heirs will also avoid paying those.

If you would like more information about the Section 1031 Exchange, I can recommend a book for you. It is called "How To Do A Section 1031 Like Kind Exchange."

Yes, I wrote it. And I also just updated it to 2018 and included the new tax law and about 70 more pages, and reduced the price.

You can find it at:

www.amazon.com/Michael-Lantrip/e/B01N2ZRGUY.

Thank you.

CHAPTER 14

ALTERNATIVE MINIMUM TAX

The Alternative Minimum Tax law requires supposedly high-income individuals to compute their tax liability twice, once using the regular tax rules, and then again using the rules of the AMT, which is a tax liability that is based on your exemptions and deductions rather than a tax on your income.

The only changes for the Alternative Minimum Tax (AMT) under the TCJA are that the exemption amounts and the phaseout thresholds are increased for individuals.

The new exemption amounts are:

- For MFJ or Surviving Spouses the amount is $109,400 instead of $84,500.

TCJA FOR REAL ESTATE INVESTORS

- For Single or Head of Household the amount is $70,300 instead of $54,300.

- For MFS the amount is $54,700 (half of the MFJ amount) instead of $42,250.

The phaseout thresholds are increased to $1M for MFJ and Surviving Spouse, and to $500,000 for everyone else.

The AMT for corporations is repealed, and the AMT rules for Trusts and Estates are unchanged.

To refresh your memory, the AMT is a tax imposed on an individual, or an estate, or a trust, based on the taxpayer's alternative minimum taxable income, referred to as AMTI.

The amount of the AMT is the excess of the taxpayer's tentative minimum tax over regular tax liability.

The tentative minimum tax is:

- 26% of the taxpayer's AMTI up to the threshold amount,

- plus 28% of AMTI over the threshold amount.

The taxpayer's AMTI is regular income increased by AMT tax preference items, and modified by AMT adjustments.

AMT tax preference items are deductions or exclusions not included in computing the AMTI.

The tax preference items are:

- Depletion.

- Intangible Drilling Costs.

- Tax-Exempt Interest from Private Activity Bonds.

- Accelerated Depreciation of Property Acquired Before 1987.

- Exclusion for Gains on Sale of Small Business Stock.

AMT adjustments are income and deduction items that are computed differently in arriving at AMTI, such as personal exemptions, the standard deduction, depreciation, NOL, and certain itemized deductions.

The complete list of adjustments that must be taken into consideration when calculating AMTI are as follows:

1.) Depreciation.

2.) Mine Exploration and Development Costs.

3.) Certain Long-Term Contracts.

4.) Pollution Control Facilities.

5.) Itemized Deductions.

6.) Standard Deductions/Exemptions.

7.) Research/Experimental Costs.

8.) Incentive Stock Plan.

9.) Passive Activity Losses.

10.) Passive Farming Activity.

11.) Net Operating Loss (NOL) Deductions.

12.) Publicly Traded Partnership (PTP).

13.) Circulation Expenses.

14.) DPAD, or Domestic Production Activities Deductions.

The Alternative Minimum Tax (AMT) law was already a mess, and it is still a mess.

When it was passed in the 1960s, it was supposed to prevent high-income taxpayers from completely avoiding the paying of individual income tax. It was "alternative," but it was not "minimum."

The tax system only worked the way it was intended for a couple of years, and then the economy improved and people were being punished who were never intended to be the target of the law.

But instead of changing it, the IRS tried to add more calculations and exceptions, until it has become almost incomprehensible. I've read cases where the Tax Court judges say they can't see how the different parts are supposed to fit together.

Anyway, we still have it, and mostly because the IRS is just reluctant to give up any taxing authority that they have fought so hard to get.

The best thing to do is to have your Tax Advisor look at your Tax Profile and warn you about which activities might trigger the Alternative Minimum Tax in your situation.

The fact that the IRS eliminated the AMT altogether for Corporations gives us some hope that it will eventually be eliminated for individual taxpayers.

CHAPTER 15

KIDDIE TAX

Many Real Estate Investors divert income to their children, both as a way to reduce their taxes, and to get the children involved in real estate investing at an early age. They do so in spite of having to deal with the dreaded "Kiddie Tax."

The so-called "Kiddie Tax" was created to prevent parents (and grandparents) in high-income tax brackets from shifting income, usually from investments, to the lower tax brackets of the children (and grandchildren).

Under the Tax Reform Act of 1986, this "unearned income" was isolated for any child to the extent that it exceeded a certain level, and instead of being taxed at the child's low tax rate, it was taxed at whatever marginal tax rate the parents were paying on their own income.

Like many things the IRS is forced to do, the solution is often worse than the problem.

Before the tax can be computed on the income attributed to the child, the parents' income tax return must be virtually completed, in order to determine that marginal tax rate. And any change or discrepancy in the parents' tax return computation could change the marginal tax rate, and change the Kiddie Tax amount on the child's tax return.

But there were still some small chances for tax savings by transferring ownership of some investments to the child and have the child file a tax return reporting the income, even if it was taxed at the parents' marginal tax rate. It was no more than the parents would be paying anyway.

The Standard Deduction in 2017 for the child declared as a Dependent on the parents' return, and for a child with no earned income, was $1,050. And the Kiddie Tax threshold was an additional $1,050.

So the child could receive up to $2,100 of unearned income without having to pay any taxes. Then, any unearned income above that amount would be taxed at the parents' marginal tax rate.

TCJA FOR REAL ESTATE INVESTORS

Under the TCJA, the "Kiddie Tax" is no longer connected to the parents' tax situation.

The TCJA leaves all of the Kiddie Tax rules in place.

The child's Standard Deduction is still $1,050.

The Kiddie Tax threshold is still $1,050.

But the new law revises the tax rate structure.

The tax has been simplified by the application of the ordinary and capital gains rates of Trusts and Estates to the unearned income of the child.

The first $2,550 of such unearned income (above the $2,100 tax-free amount) is taxed at only 10%. If the income is in the nature of Long-term Capital Gains or Qualified Dividends, it might even qualify for the 0% rate. That would mean that the parents can shift $4,650 of tax-free income to the child.

For the next $6,600 of unearned income, the tax rate is 24%.

This is the point at which the tax strategy might start losing its appeal.

But the parents might still pay the child to work in the business and pay a wage or a fee for personal services rendered.

This income would not be unearned income like the interest, dividends, and capital gains.

This would be earned income, and would be taxed under the tax brackets and rates of a single taxpayer, and not subject to the Kiddie Tax.

CHAPTER 16

NET OPERATING LOSS

Real Estate Investors with large amounts of Depreciation often create significant Net Operating Loss (NOL) in the operation of the business.

There are two very important changes in the NOL rules in the Tax Cuts And Jobs Act.

Your NOL has always been calculated as the amount by which your total business deductions exceed your gross income for the tax year.

The actual computation is actually far more complicated than this, and Internal Revenue Code Section 172(d) lists various modifications that the taxpayer, both corporate and individual, must take into account in calculating the actual amount of NOL that will be allowed to be claimed on the Taxpayer's current year tax return.

Under the old law, if the Taxpayer had NOL that could not be claimed on the current year's tax return, the Taxpayer was permitted to "carryback" the NOL for two years and apply it to that already-filed tax return, and file a Form 1040X Amended Tax Return, and probably receive a tax refund based on the reduction of taxable income.

If all of the NOL was not used up in that transaction, the remaining NOL could then be applied to the prior year's return, and that return could also be amended.

Once the two-year "carryback" had been used up, the remaining NOL, if any, could be carried forward for as long as 20 years, at which point any unused amount would just expire.

There were exceptions to these time periods.

For instance, REITs could not carry the NOL back at all, but could still carry it forward for the 20-year period.

If the NOL was for an individual and it came about due to a fire, storm, theft, shipwreck, or other casualty, the carryback period was three years.

TCJA FOR REAL ESTATE INVESTORS

And yes, IRC Section 172(b)(1)(E)(ii)(1) actually covers shipwrecks.

Also, the carryback period is three years instead of two for a small business or taxpayer in a farming activity if the NOL is the result of a federally-declared disaster.

For regular farming losses resulting in an NOL, the carryback period is five years. There is a specific calculation for determining the farming loss, and the farmer is required to make an election regarding how the NOL will be used.

And there is even a 10-year carryback period for special liability losses, which is the portion of an NOL that is attributable to product liability, or to the satisfaction of a liability under federal or state law requiring land reclamation, nuclear power plant decommissioning, drilling platform dismantling, environmental remediation, or a payment under any workers' compensation act.

If a taxpayer is qualified under the NOL rules as of December 31, 2017, then the taxpayer will continue to be subject to those rules, and will not have to conform to the TCJA arrangement.

Under the new tax law, there are two major changes.

The first one is that, except for some farming losses and casualty losses described below, the carryback provisions are completely eliminated.

NOLs can no longer be carried back.

And, along with that, the carryforward provisions are no longer limited to 20 years, but go on indefinitely, for as long as there is an NOL balance to be applied.

For Taxpayers who use a non-calendar tax year, the first year of filing is tricky, so if you are a Taxpayer who used a tax year other than the calendar year you will have to turn to a tax professional for a breakdown of how the new law will affect you during their first year of filing.

The second major change is that only 80% of the available NOL amount can be used to offset taxable income in the year in which it is applied.

So, let's look at next year, the 2019 tax year.

If you are carrying $100,000 of NOL into next year, and you end up with $120,000 of taxable income, you can only use $96,000 of NOL, because this is 80% of your taxable income. The remaining $4,000 of the $100,000 must be carried forward to the next year.

TCJA FOR REAL ESTATE INVESTORS

If your taxable income is $40,000 instead of $120,000 you can only offset $32,000 of the taxable income with your available NOL. And the remaining $68,000 balance of the NOL must be carried forward.

However, if you are a taxpayer with NOL carryforward from prior to 2018 when the TCJA became effective, you can use your old NOL to offset your remaining taxable income, because old NOL is not subject to the 80% rule.

The 80% rule also applies to REITs, but there are special calculations that are explained in IRC Section 172(d)(6)(C).

As mentioned above, the five-year carryback period for farm losses has been eliminated, but has been replaced with a two-year carryback period. There are special conditions and procedures for this and they are explained in IRC Section 172(b)(1)(B).

The other difference for farmers is that the two-year carryback period is also subject to the 80% limitation, but still contains the opt-out option.

With the new 20% deduction for Qualified Business Income (QBI), the question now becomes whether "taxable income" means before the 20% QBI deduction, or after.

And the answer is that "taxable income" means total taxable income before any deduction is taken for the 20% QBI provision.

So, if all of your taxable income is QBI, and you have enough NOL carryforward, you could eliminate 80% of it with the NOL and the other 20% of it with the QBI deduction, and all of your income could be tax-free.

For individual Taxpayers who are not Corporations, see Chapter 17, Excess Business Losses.

CHAPTER 17

EXCESS BUSINESS LOSSES

Non-Corporate Taxpayers, including:

1.) individuals,

2.) partners, and

3.) S Corp shareholders

have always had limitations on their deductions allowed on their tax return caused by losses from their trade or business activities.

The limitations could be tied to:

1.) net operating losses (NOLs),

2.) passive activity loss limitations,

3.) at risk issues, or

4.) basis in property issues.

Now the new Tax Cuts And Jobs Act has added something called "Excess Business Loss" for Non-Corporate Taxpayers.

It is defined as:

"The amount by which the Taxpayer's aggregate deductions attributable to the Taxpayer's trades or businesses exceeds the aggregate gross income and/or gains attributable to those trades or businesses, plus another $250,000 (or $500,000 for MFJ) of hypothetical income."

This income, gain, deduction, or loss for S Corp shareholders and Partners in a Partnership will be reported to them on their Schedule K-1.

The losses above the amount not allowed must be treated the same as a Net Operating Losses (NOL) and they must be carried forward under the carryforward rules that apply to NOLs.

But before applying the rules for the Excess Business Loss (EBL), you must first assess whether the "passive activity loss" (PAL) rules also apply.

Under the PAL rules, losses and expenses attributable to passive activities can only be deducted from income that is also derived from passive activities.

In other words, profit from non-passive activities cannot be reduced by PAL.

"Passive activity" is defined as any trade or business activity in which the taxpayer owns an interest, but does not "materially participate."

"Materially participate" means different things depending on what the activity is, and how much "participation" it requires to operate the enterprise properly.

But then the definition does not apply to rental activities because these have been determined by the IRS to be passive activities regardless of whether the taxpayer "materially participates" in the activity.

And the PAL rules don't just apply to individuals. They also apply to trusts, estates, corporations that are personal service corporations, and C corporations that are closely held corporations.

The rules do not apply to S Corps and Partnerships, but, of course, when the losses and credits from these entities are passed through to the owners on the K-1, the rules then apply to those taxpayers.

If all of the taxpayer's PAL exceeds all of the taxpayer's passive activity income, the excess amount is classified as Excess Business Losses (EBL) and must be carried forward until the taxpayer has some passive activity income to offset.

Excess farm losses are subject to special rules.

The EBL that is carried forward as an NOL are subject to the 80% limitation for NOLs in effect under the new TCJA.

CHAPTER 18

CONCLUSION

Real Estate is poised for the biggest growth cycle in thirty years after passage of the Tax Cuts And Jobs Act, and the big winners will be the first Real Estate Investors to learn the new rules.

The Real Estate Investing decisions that you made last year will probably be the wrong ones to make this year.

For Example, the 20% income exclusion for PTEs will affect every real estate investing decision made from this point forward, including yours, and you need to understand completely how it works.

This is a whole new world of Real Estate Investing, and the quicker you learn the new rules, the quicker you will build your system.

But remember that this is just the beginning.

I was an active Real Estate Investor and Attorney during the last major tax law overhaul, and it took about three years before we were in a position where it had morphed into its final form. I filed quite a few amended tax returns.

Then the Tax Court cases and the Federal District Court cases started coming down, and we made more adjustments.

So keep in mind, there will be changes.

The Treasury Regulations have not yet been written. They will explain what the law actually means, and they will contain Examples that we can work through.

But it really looks great for Real Estate Investors, and that will not change.

There will also be big changes on the state level.

We are probably in the historical era of the development of two very separate tax systems: federal and state.

TCJA FOR REAL ESTATE INVESTORS

Before passage of the Tax Cuts And Jobs Act, most states had the same tax treatment for many of the items of income and deductions as those of the IRS.

But since the passage of TCJA, a number of states have also passed new laws that "decouple" parts of their state tax system from the federal tax system.

More states are expected to follow suit.

We should know more about this within the next two years.

MICHAEL LANTRIP

BONUS

The following material contains 14 chapters of "50 Real Estate Investing Calculations" published in December of last year in both print and digital.

Please read the Introduction for an explanation of what Calculations are, and how to use them.

In the Contents section, you can see the remainder of the 50 Calculations in the book.

I hope that you enjoy these 14, and that you benefit from them.

If you want more information, please visit my Author Page at Amazon.

www.amazon.com/Michael-Lantrip/e/B01N2ZRGUY.

INTRODUCTION

This book is not a promise that you will make money investing in real estate, or an explanation of how to do it.

There are other books for that.

This book is a presentation of all of the Calculations that you must understand in order to see the dynamics that are controlling real estate investing, and controlling whether or not you will make a profit.

These Calculations are actually the Set Of Rules in the world of Real Estate Investing.

Whether you know the Calculations or not, they are at work behind the scenes determining whether you will be profitable and successful, or out of business in a year.

I have selected 50 of them, and I will provide a separate Section for each Calculation. About 15 of them you have not seen before.

Most of the Calculations are very simple to do. A few are complicated. And all of them that you have seen are usually over-explained to the point of confusion. And some of them are just being done incorrectly, by including the wrong items. I'll explain how and why, and let you decide.

But if you can add, subtract, multiply and divide, you can do these Calculations.

The important thing is to understand:

- the origin of the numbers you are putting into the Calculation, and

- the meaning of the number produced by the Calculation.

I will explain both in detail.

The Calculations are all related to each other in some manner, because they all relate to the same thing, the investment property.

So, in discussing each of the Calculations it will be necessary to repeat some of the information from other Sections. It is easier than having you refer back and forth between Sections.

TCJA FOR REAL ESTATE INVESTORS

You can read the Sections in any order that is convenient for you.

Just remember that understanding the Real Estate Investing Calculations is like looking behind the walls and seeing how the model is built.

You will see the foundation, framing, wiring, plumbing, and everything else that causes Real Estate Investing to behave the way it does.

You will become the Master Builder of your investment portfolio once you can understand and use these Calculations.

I will also provide you with 24 Free Calculators that I think you will find useful for doing quick Calculations, and then for trying other combinations to see how you might find a better ratio.

Real Estate Investing Calculations are the way that you measure and manage your investments.

Period!

Good Luck!

SECTION 1.

APPRECIATION

"Appreciation" is the term applied to the increase in value of your investment property.

Of course, if you've owned the investment property for a period of time, you can determine the increase in value by subtracting the Original Value from the Present Value.

To determine the percentage of Appreciation, you divide the Appreciation by the Original Value.

A = (PV − OV) ÷ OV, WHERE

A IS THE APPRECIATION PERCENTAGE,

PV IS THE PRESENT VALUE, AND

OV IS THE ORIGINAL VALUE

For Example, you bought a Fourplex for $400,000 a year ago and now you have determined by using the market Capitalization Rate for this type of property that it now has a value of $426,800.

$$A = (PV - OV) \div OV$$

$$A = (426{,}800 - 400{,}000) \div 400{,}000$$

$$A = 26{,}800 \div 400{,}000$$

$$A = 0.067 = 6.7\%$$

The investment property has appreciated in value 6.7% in one year.

FUTURE VALUE

But we are usually interested in determining the Appreciation that will occur in investment property that we are considering purchasing.

For this, we use the Future Value Calculation.

FV = PV x (1+ I), WHERE

FV IS THE FUTURE VALUE,

PV IS THE PRESENT VALUE,

1 IS 1, AND

I IS THE PERCENTAGE INCREASE FACTOR.

For Example, we buy a $400,000 Fourplex and expect it to increase in value 6.7% each year.

$FV = PV \times (1 + I)$

$FV = 400,000 \times (1 + .067)$

$FV = 400,000 \times 1.067$

$FV = 426,800$

At the end of Year 1, your Fourplex will have appreciated in value to $426,800.

Now, for the Calculation on the second and subsequent years' appreciation, you use a new PV figure for the ending of the prior year, which is the same as the beginning of the current year.

In this Example for the second year we would use a PV of $426,800 because that is what it was at the end of the first year.

$FV = PV \times (1 + I)$

$FV = 426,800 \times 1.067$

$FV = 455,396$

At the end of your second year of ownership, your Fourplex will have appreciated to a value of $455,396.

Alternatively, you could multiply 1.067 times 1.067 and get 1.1385, and multiply 1.1385 times 400,000 and get the same number: 455,396.

See SECTION 26. FUTURE VALUE for more information, and a link to a Free Calculator to use:

https://www.calculatorsoup.com/calculators/financial/future-value-calculator-basic.php

EQUITY

The above Calculation will serve you well if you pay cash for the investment property, but few of us do. We usually have debt on the property.

If you have debt on the property, then what you actually have that is appreciating in value is more than just the Fair Market Value (FMV) of the property.

What you have that is actually appreciating in value is your Equity in the property.

There is a Calculation for Equity.

E = FMV − MPO − L − OD, where

E is your Equity in the property,

FMV is the Fair Market Value of the property,

MPO is the Mortgage Payoff amount,

L is Liens on the property, and

OD is Other Debts on the property

A month after you purchase the property, the FMV will already have gone up, because that is what property does, and the MPO will go down, because each of your mortgage payments will be a combination of interest and reduction of principal. The reduction of principal amount will reduce your MPO. The reduction will be small at the beginning, and huge at the end.

If you want to Calculate your probable Equity in the future, you would use the Future Value Calculation to determine the new amount of the FMV, and then use your Amortization Schedule for your mortgage payments that you received from your lender to get your Mortgage Payoff amount for the specific date you are calculating for.

Then plug the two numbers into the above Equity Calculation to determine your Equity at any point.

See SECTION 24. EQUITY for more information.

VALUE AND CAPITALIZATION RATE

It is important that you have an accurate number for the "value" factor in the Calculations.

The best number to use is the actual selling price of comparable properties in your market.

But if you do not know what these are, or do not have enough comparable sales, or your property is unique, then you can still Calculate a figure for Value.

See SECTION 50. VALUE.

That Calculation will require you to also Calculate a Capitalization Rate, referred to as the Cap Rate.

See SECTION 10. CAPITALIZATION RATE.

SECTION 2.

BALANCE SHEET

A Balance Sheet is normally done for a company, showing the company Assets, the company Liabilities, and the company Net Worth.

It can also be done for a business activity, or a single real estate project, or real estate investment.

You can even do it for your personal finances.

A Balance Sheet is a snapshot of the specific entity or activity at a specific point in time, and covering a specific time period.

The time chosen is usually the end of the year, or the end of one of the quarters.

This is what a Balance Sheet looks like:

TCJA FOR REAL ESTATE INVESTORS

ABC COMPANY
Anytown, USA
March 31, 2018

ASSETS

CURRENT ASSETS

Cash	9,000	
Accounts Receivable	3,140	
Quarterly Tax Deposits	8,000	
Prepaid Expenses	1,270	
TOTAL CURRENT ASSETS		21,410

LONG-TERM ASSETS

Land	45,000	
Building	360,000	
Accum. Dep.	(71,280)	
	288,720	
Fix. & Equip.	38,000	
Accum. Dep.	(9,441)	
	28,559	
TOTAL LONG-TERM ASSETS		362,279

MICHAEL LANTRIP

OTHER ASSETS

Security Deposits	1,400
Notes Receivable	1,160
TOTAL OTHER ASSETS	**2,560**

TOTAL ASSETS   **386,249**

LIABILITIES

CURRENT LIABILITIES

Accounts Payable	9,750
Sales Taxes Accrued	1,450
TOTAL CURRENT LIABILITIES	**11,200**

LONG-TERM LIABILITIES

Mortgages	272,544
Notes Payable	1,750
TOTAL LONG-TERM LIABILITIES	**274,294**

TOTAL LIABILITIES   **285,494**

NET WORTH   **100,755**

Often, an Income Statement is done at the same time to accompany the Balance Sheet.

See SECTION 27. INCOME STATEMENT.

The Calculation for a Balance Sheet is:

$A = L + N$, or (more helpfully)

$N = A - L$, where

N is Net Worth,

A is total Assets, and

L is total Liabilities

Net Worth is sometimes also called "Equity," but this is not correct.

The Calculation for Equity is:

$E = FMV - MPO - L - OD$, where

E is your Equity in the property,

FMV is the Fair Market Value of the property,

MPO is the total amount of your Mortgage Payoff,

L is the Liens on the property, and

OD is Other Debt on the property

Notice that the Value of the property is the FMV. That is what the property will sell for on the open market today.

In the Balance Sheet, the FMV is not used. The Value that is used on the Balance Sheet is the Depreciated Book Value. That number is much lower, and will not tell you what your Equity is.

The "Equity" or "Owner's Equity" terms that are often used in reference to a Balance Sheet should be avoided in favor of using the term "Net Worth."

But, like "Equity," the term "Net Worth" also does not accurately describe what it is.

Net Worth is just the difference between the Book Value of the company assets, and the total amount of your Liabilities. It's just a number. It does not tell you the total value of the company.

SECTION 3.

BASIS

If you own real estate, you have a "Basis" in that property.

There are three ways that your Basis (B) in property comes into existence.

1.) You bought the property.

2.) You received the property as a gift, or

3.) You inherited the property.

PURCHASED PROPERTY

If you bought the property, your Basis is what you paid for the property.

If you've made any capital improvements to the property, this amount is added to your Basis, unless you identify the improvements separately and depreciate them on your Depreciation Schedule.

Internal Revenue Code (IRC) Section 1012, entitled "Basis of Property – Cost," says simply that "The basis of property shall be the cost of such property..."

It goes on to cover specific and unusual situations, but "Cost Basis" is the general rule for purchased property.

Today, if you purchased a Duplex for $265,000 your Basis in that property is what you paid for it, plus any acquisition costs, usually closing costs.

If you incurred $5,000 in acquisition costs, then your Basis in the property is $270,000.

If you spend $30,000 improving the property, then your Basis in the property becomes $300,000.

If you sell at this point, your Capital Gains will be the differences between your $300,000 Basis and your Net Sales Proceeds.

If you rent out the property, you will be allowed to claim an annual depreciation allowance, and deduct that amount from your rental income, and this Depreciation will lower your Basis in the property.

TCJA FOR REAL ESTATE INVESTORS

See Sections 14 through 23 on Depreciation for complete explanations of the Calculations involved in the process of doing Depreciation.

But let's assume that you assign a value of $25,000 to the land, and subtract that out because land is not subject to depreciation.

That leaves a Depreciable Basis in the property of $275,000 which can be depreciated over a period of 27.5 years, resulting in an annual depreciation allowance of $10,000. (Yes, I manipulated the numbers. Did you see it coming?)

After you have rented the Duplex for five years and claimed $50,000 in depreciation allowance, your Basis in the property is $250,000 because you must deduct Depreciation from your Basis.

So, for property that you purchased, your Basis is the purchase price, plus cost of improvements, and minus depreciation allowed.

B = PP + CI − D, where:

B is the Basis in the Property,

PP is the Purchase Price,

CI is the Cost of Improvements, and

D is the Depreciation allowed.

For our Example above:

B = 270,000 + 30,000 − 50,000

B = 250,000

GIFTED PROPERTY

If you received property as a gift, your Basis in the property will be the same as the Basis of the individual who gifted the property to you.

See SECTION 7. BASIS: TRANSFERRED for more details.

INHERITED PROPERTY

If you inherited property, you might or might not receive a Step-up in Basis.

See SECTION 6. BASIS: STEPPED-UP for an explanation.

SECTION 4.

BASIS: ADJUSTED

Your "Basis" in your property is what you paid for it, plus any capital improvements you have made.

Your "Adjusted Basis" in your property is the basis adjusted for the Depreciation that you have taken. In other words, the book value less the depreciation deduction.

Adjusted Basis is also referred to as "Depreciated Basis."

In fact, your Balance Sheet for your investment will be divided by Assets and Liabilities.

Under Assets, you will see your major assets listed separately, with the price that you paid, or the price allocated for each.

Then you will see an entry underneath called "Accumulated Depreciation," and a number, and then you will see another figure.

This other figure is your Adjusted Basis. It is the amount paid for the property less any depreciation taken.

For Example, let's assume that you purchase a Duplex for $240,000 and have $10,000 closing costs. You then spend $25,000 on improvements, and you hold the investment for three years and consider selling it. What is your Capital Gains?

The first thing you need to know in order to answer this question will be the number for your Adjusted Basis.

Your total cost to start with is $275,000.

This is the total of your Purchase Price, your Closing Costs, and your Capital Improvements.

During the three years, you have claimed $9,091 in Depreciation each year, for a total of $27,273.

You subtract the $27,273 from the $275,000 and you have your Adjusted Basis. That number is $247,727.

TCJA FOR REAL ESTATE INVESTORS

There are other situations which might result in an Adjusted Basis for your asset, such as a casualty loss (fire) for which you were reimbursed by insurance.

In this case, you deduct the amount of your insurance check from your Basis, and this is your new Adjusted Basis.

But in most cases, your Adjusted Basis will only be the result of the amount of your depreciation taken.

CALCULATOR

Now that you understand how this works, let's run it through a Free Calculator and see what we get.

https://www.ajdesigner.com/php_ab/adjusted_basis.php

- For "original basis (OB)" enter 250000 (no comma).

- For "Capital additions (CA)" enter 25000.

- For "sales costs (SC)" enter 0.

- For "cumulative real estate depreciation (CRED)" enter 27273.

- For "cumulative capital improvements depreciation (CCAD)" enter 2727.

- Click "Calculate."

Your Adjusted Basis is $245,000.

This is a different number from the one we got above because we did not account for the value of the land.

This Calculator also allows you how to calculate for any of the elements when you know all of the others.

Just click on that Calculation in the box and the screen will give you a different Calculation page.

SECTION 5.

BASIS: CARRYOVER

Carryover Basis (CB) is often mistakenly referred to as Transferred Basis (TB).

The two are not the same.

See SECTION 7. BASIS: TRANSFERRED for a full explanation of how that comes about and what it is.

Generally when property is gifted from one person, called the donor, to another person, called the donee, the Basis that the donor has in the property is transferred to the donee, becoming the Transferred Basis.

But Carryover Basis is when there is a business transaction involving two pieces of property, one being sold and one being purchased, by a single investor, and the Basis of the sold property carries over into the Basis of the purchased property.

An Example of this would be a Section 1031 Like Kind Exchange.

You bought a Duplex ten years ago for $200,000 and have operated it as an investment property. You have claimed $65,000 in Depreciation during that time.

Now you are selling the Duplex for $400,000 and you are buying a Replacement Property of equal or greater value, engaging in a Section 1031 Like Kind Exchange in order to avoid paying taxes on the Capital Gains and the Depreciation Recapture.

You paid $200,000 for the Duplex and you claimed $65,000 in Depreciation, which is deducted from the beginning Basis of $200,000, leaving a Basis of $135,000.

Under the provisions of Section 1031, you are allowed to take the $135,000 of Basis that you have left in the Duplex that you have not yet depreciated, and carry it over into the Replacement Property, and continue to claim Depreciation on it, even though you no longer own it.

And this Basis is called Carryover Basis.

All in all, a pretty great deal.

By the way, if you are interested in learning more about the Section 1031 Like Kind Exchange, I can highly recommend an excellent book on the subject.

"How To Do A Section 1031 Like Kind Exchange" is available on Amazon, and you can do a "Look Inside" at:

amazon.com/Michael-Lantrip/e/B01N2ZRGUY

SECTION 6.

BASIS: STEPPED-UP

FOR INDIVIDUAL TAXPAYERS

A step-up in Basis happens when the property owner dies, and the property is inherited either through the probate of a Will or the administration of an intestate estate, or the property goes into a trust.

Internal Revenue Code Section 1014, entitled "Basis Of Property Acquired From A Decedent," provides that the Basis of a Decedent's property will be changed (usually increased) to its Fair Market Value (FMV) as of the Date of Death (DOD).

IRC Section 1014(a) says "... the basis of property in the hands of a person acquiring the property from a decedent or to whom the property passed from a decedent shall, if not sold, exchanged, or otherwise disposed of before the decedent's death by such person, be (1) the fair market value of the property at the date of decedent's death, ..."

It can be confusing, but it just means that there is a step-up in Basis when a person dies and leaves property to an heir.

The step-up in Basis will usually mean that the person inheriting the property can sell it without having to pay any Capital Gains Tax because the sale will usually be for the FMV, and the seller's Basis in the property is also the FMV, because that is what the step-up in Basis does, raise the Basis to the FMV.

The real value of the Stepped-up Basis comes from using Section 1031 Exchanges for your entire lifetime to defer the Capital Gains taxes, and then passing your property to your heirs.

You might have started with an investment in a property with a Basis of $50,000 and, through a series of Section 1031 Exchanges, now have property worth $1,000,000 but with a Basis of less than $100,000.

With a Capital Gains rate of 20%, the step-up in Basis will avoid a tax bill of about $180,000.

After deferring taxes on Capital Gains and Depreciation Recapture for your entire life, the "pot of gold at the end of the rainbow" is to pass the property to your heirs, and eliminate all of your tax liability.

Stepped-up Basis turns the "tax-deferred" taxes from all of your past sales into "tax-free" for your heirs.

However, it matters whether you are holding title to the property in your own name, or you own the property through a business entity.

You might still be entitled to claim a Stepped-up Basis if you hold the property through a business entity, but it will depend on the business entity in which you are holding the property.

FOR BUSINESS ENTITIES

If you are not holding real property in your own name, then Partnerships and LLCs are the best business entities to use.

The LLC can elect for tax purposes to be treated as either a disregarded entity, a partnership or an S Corp. But it should not be treated as a C Corp.

TCJA FOR REAL ESTATE INVESTORS

By taking an Internal Revenue Code Section 754 election upon the death of a shareholder, the Partnership or LLC gets a step-up in Basis for the property in the hands of the beneficiary.

For Example, let's assume that you and your brother set up a corporation and each of you put in $50,000 and each of you own 50% of the stock. The corporation buys a warehouse for $100,000.

Ten years later, you die and leave everything to your son, and the warehouse is worth $1,000,000.

Your son will receive a Stepped-up Basis in the value of the corporate stock.

But the corporation will not receive a Stepped-up Basis in the value of the warehouse. The warehouse is owned by the corporation, and the corporation did not die. If the warehouse is sold, the corporation will owe taxes on $900,000 of Capital Gains. (Including an undeterminable amount for Depreciation Recapture Tax). In effect, your son will pay half of the taxes because it will come out of his half of the corporation's funds.

Now, let's assume that you and your brother set up an LLC instead of a corporation, and that everything else is the same. The LLC will be treated for tax purposes as a Partnership because there is more than one owner.

When you die, the LLC makes a Section 754 election, and the son's share of the LLC assets receives a Stepped-up Basis to $500,000.

If the LLC sells the warehouse, the son will have no Capital Gains taxes to pay. If the LLC does not sell the warehouse, the son has a Basis of $500,000 inside the LLC which he can depreciate.

FOR HUSBANDS AND WIVES

If a Husband and Wife own the real estate together, the survivor will receive a Stepped-up Basis in the share owned by the deceased spouse, but may not receive a Stepped-up Basis in their own share upon the death of the spouse.

It will depend on the state in which they live, and the manner in which they are holding title to the property.

If the real estate is held in Joint Tenancy, and one spouse dies, the surviving spouse will received a Stepped-up Basis in the share of the property inherited from the deceased spouse, but will not receive a Stepped-up Basis in the share of the property that was already owned. This share retains its Cost Basis.

But in Community Property states, the opposite is true.

If the surviving spouse inherits the property, all of the property receives a Stepped-up Basis.

In our Example of a $300,000 property, if the Community Property surviving spouse sold it shortly after the death of her spouse for $500,000, there would be no Capital Gains tax because the Sales Price would be the same as the Stepped-up Basis.

But if the Joint Tenancy surviving spouse did the same, her Basis in the property would be $150,000, half of the Cost Basis of $300,000, plus $250,000, the Stepped-up Basis of the share of the deceased spouse, for a total Basis of $400,000.

The Joint Tenancy surviving spouse would have a $100,000 Capital Gains tax liability.

(These Examples ignore allowable depreciation.)

Community Property states are Arizona, California, Idaho, Louisiana, Nevada, New Mexico, Texas, Washington, and Wisconsin.

Alaska allows spouses to opt-in to a Community Property arrangement.

SECTION 7.

BASIS: TRANSFERRED

If you receive property as a gift, your Basis (B) in the property will be the same as the Basis of the individual who gifted the property to you.

The Basis is "transferred" to you and is called Transferred Basis (TB).

Internal Revenue Code Section 1015, entitled "Basis of Property Acquired By Gifts And Transfers In Trust," says "If the property was acquired by gift ... the basis shall be the same as it would be in the hands of a donor or the last preceding owner by whom it was not acquired by gift, except that if such basis ... is greater than the fair market value of the property at the time of the gift, then for the purpose of determining loss the basis shall be such fair market value."

For Example, a mistake often made by elderly parents regarding their real property is that they want to gift it to their children before they die so that it will not have to go through Probate.

Here's the problem with that.

They might have property worth $400,000 that they have owned all of their lives and in which they might have a very low Basis, or no Basis at all due to Depreciation taken.

If it is gifted to the children, when the children sell it, they will have a Capital Gains tax on the entire $400,000, possibly as high as 20%, because they have no Basis in the property, or very low Basis, because their Basis is the same as the Basis of the parents who gifted the property.

This is Transferred Basis.

For an explanation of what would happen if the situation were handled differently, perhaps putting the property into a Revocable Living Trust that becomes Irrevocable upon death, see SECTION 6. BASIS: STEPPED-UP.

Also, note that Transferred Basis is often also referred to as Carryover Basis, but the two are not the same.

See the SECTION 5. BASIS: CARRYOVER for a full explanation.

SECTION 8.

CAPITAL EXPENDITURES

Capital Expenditures (Cap Ex) is a category that includes those major repairs such as a roof, furnace, HVAC system, or foundation that will happen if you own the investment property long enough.

A roof replacement is not a monthly expenditure to be deducted from cash income to determine Cash Flow (CF), until it happens.

When it does happen, you are faced with trying to deduct a $25,000 expense from $1,000 of available income that month to calculate CF.

Of course, that Calculation of minus $24,000 is worthless, and renders all of the previous Cash Flows worthless, because Cap Ex is supposed to be part of your CF calculations, and you have not been deducting an allowance for Cap Ex.

The Cap Ex is really an expenditure that should be deducted over the life of the item that failed.

Spreading it out this way gives you a true Calculation of what your CF actually is, or will be, if you are doing a CF projection.

But how do you do this?

Well, you can do it the easy way, or you can do it the hard way.

The easy way is to look at your Depreciation Schedule and see what assets you are depreciating.

You will have a building, called Section 1250 Property, that you are depreciating in a straight-line method over a period of 27.5 years if it is Residential Real Estate, and 39 years if it is Commercial Real Estate.

For Example, you have a Duplex with a Fair Market Value (FMV) of $185,000.

TCJA FOR REAL ESTATE INVESTORS

You assign $20,000 to the value of the land, leaving $165,000 value in the building available for depreciation.

Divide that by 27.5 years and you can claim $6,000 per year in Depreciation, or $500 per month.

Let's say you are also depreciating personal property as part of the package, called Section 1245 Property, and using one of the Accelerated Depreciation methods such as Double Declining Balance (DDB).

Your initial monthly depreciation amounts will be large, and decline over the life of the asset.

But you can smooth that out by just taking the total value of the Section 1245 Property and divide it by the life of the assets.

If you have $15,000 of such property with a depreciable life of 5 years, or 60 months, then use $250 as the average of monthly claimed Depreciation.

Your total claimed Depreciation, both Section 1250 Property and Section 1245 Property, is $750 per month.

You might choose to use this amount as your monthly estimate for Cap Ex.

Doing it this way will give you two advantages.

The first is that it saves a lot of time, because the number already exists.

The second is that it will also allow you to track your Taxable Income (TI) at the same time.

Taxable Income is just your CF with Cap Ex added back to it, and then Depreciation and Mortgage Interest (MI) subtracted.

Using the same numbers for Cap Ex and Depreciation make them a wash.

You can take your monthly CF number and subtract MI, and you have a good estimate of your TI.

The other way, the hard way, involves actually listing all of the components that could cause a major expense to occur, the roof, the HVAC system, the furnace, the foundation, etc.

You identify how much it would cost to replace each one, the Replacement Cost (RC).

Then you look at the charts that show how long each one would last, and estimate how much of that life is left remaining for each of your items.

Divide the remaining life into the RC and you have a yearly Cap Ex amount for that item, the eventual cost of replacing the item spread over its remaining life.

For Example, a 25-year roof that would cost $25,000 to replace, and which you estimate has a remaining life of 18 years would create a Cap Ex figure of $104.16 per month.

When you have done this for all of the major components, you will have a Cap Ex figure to use in your CF estimate that will help you avoid the disaster of losing you entire investment because of one large repair.

If you do not suffer any large repairs while you own the property, you have that Cap Ex fund as a bonus when you sell.

SECTION 9.

CAPITAL GAINS

Let's start simple.

Capital Gain, basically, is the profit that you make when you sell your investment property.

From there, it becomes more complex.

Your Capital Gains is the difference between what you paid for your property and what you sold the property for.

Except that there are some adjustments to be made.

First, you can deduct all or most of the costs of transaction from the selling price. Usually, you will have these charges listed on your HUD-1 Settlement

Statement. Also, there might be some expenses that were paid outside of closing that were actually expenses of the sale.

That takes care of the amount that you received for the property, your Net Sales Proceeds.

Now, what you deduct from your Net Sales Proceeds is called your Adjusted Basis in the property.

See SECTION 3. BASIS and SECTION 4. BASIS: ADJUSTED for a full explanation of this.

But for now, a quick description of your Adjusted Basis in the property is the amount that you paid for the property, plus any capital improvements made to the property, and minus any depreciation claimed on the property.

CG = NSP – OPP + CI – D, WHERE

CG IS CAPITAL GAINS,

NSP IS YOUR NET SALES PRICE,

OPP IS YOUR ORIGINAL PURCHASE PRICE,

CI IS CAPITAL IMPROVEMENTS, AND

D IS DEPRECIATION TAKEN

For Example, you purchased a Duplex ten years ago for $200,000. You added two garages for $30,000 and replaced the furniture and fixtures for $20,000.

You have taken $65,000 Depreciation on the Duplex and you have taken $8,000 Depreciation on the garages, and you have taken $15,000 Depreciation on the furniture and fixtures.

Now you sell the Duplex for $400,000 and have $10,000 in transaction costs.

CG = NSP − OPP + CI − D

CG = (400,000 − 10,000) − [200,000 + (30,000 + 20,000) − (65,000 + 8,000 + 15,000)]

CG = 390,000 − (200,000 + 50,000 − 88,000)

CG = 390,000 − 162,000

CG = 228,000

Your Capital Gains on that transaction is $228,000.

If you had held the property for one year or less, the Capital Gains would be classified as Short-Term Capital Gains.

Short-Term Capital Gains is taxed at the same rate as your personal ordinary income tax rate for the tax year in which the transaction took place.

But you held the property for at least a year and a day, so the Capital Gains is classified as Long-Term Capital Gains.

Long-Term Capital Gains is taxed at different rates for different taxpayers, depending on the amount of their other income, ranging from 0% to 20%.

But part of your Capital Gains will be taxed at the Capital Gains tax rate, and part of it will be taxed as Depreciation Recapture, and at what will probably be a higher rate.

See SECTION 23. DEPRECIATION RECAPTURE for a full explanation.

SECTION 10.

CAPITALIZATION RATE

The Capitalization Rate (CR), referred to as the Cap Rate, is the ratio of the Net Operating Income (NOI) to the Fair Market Value (FMV) of the property.

The CR is your overall rate of return on the value of the asset.

CR = NOI ÷ FMV, where

CR is the Cap Rate,

NOI is the Net Operating Income, and

FMV is the Fair Market Value of the property.

For Example, if you have a $500,000 multi-family property that has a Net Operating Income of $65,000 the Calculation is:

CR = NOI ÷ FMV

CR = 65,000 ÷ 500,000

CR = 0.13

The Cap Rate for this property is 13%.

Investors in a particular market, or for a particular type of real estate investment, don't actually declare what their Cap Rate is, but they establish the Cap Rate by their decisions on how much to pay for an investment property that has a specific Net Operating Income.

In the above Example, investors in that market are willing to pay $500,000 for an investment property that has Net Operating Income of $65,000. That consensus among them creates the 13% factor as the market Cap Rate for property of that specific type in that specific price range in that specific market.

The Law of Supply And Demand will create the consensus.

So, you will hear references that say the Cap Rate is such-and-such for this type of property in this market.

One of the values of using the Cap Rate to compare different properties is that the NOI does not include debt service, an expense which will be different for every potential buyer, and using the Cap Rate allows for across-the-board comparisons of just the properties, with the same assumptions applied to each one.

In addition to using the Cap Rate alone to compare potential investment properties, you can use it in association with Cash Flow analysis.

A calculation based on Cap Rate and Discounted Cash Flow might give you even more valuable information.

CALCULATOR

You can quickly Calculate your Cap Rate with the following Free Calculator.

https://www.ajdesigner.com/php_capitalization_rate/capitalization_rate.php

- For "net operating income (NOI)" enter 65000 (no comma).

TCJA FOR REAL ESTATE INVESTORS

- For "value or cost (V)" enter 500000.
- Click "Calculate."

Your Cap Rate is 13%.

This is the same number that we got when doing it by hand.

SECTION 11.

CASH FLOW

Cash Flow is easy to Calculate for property you already own, and almost impossible to Calculate for property that you are thinking about buying.

Cash Flow is the cash left over after you take the monthly income from the property and pay all of the monthly expenses of the property.

In other words, it is cash in, less cash out.

CF = I – E, where

CF is Cash Flow,

I is all of the cash Income, and

E is all of the cash Expenses.

TCJA FOR REAL ESTATE INVESTORS

Although you will read otherwise, "Expenses" as the term is used in Cash Flow analysis does not include Debt Service (DS) because that is not one of the characteristics of the property that you are analyzing.

After all, the purpose of calculating Cash Flow in the first place is to determine if there will be enough to make the monthly payments on the loan to purchase it.

Your Lender wants to see the Cash Flow from the operation of the property to see if you will be able to make the note payments, and cover other contingencies (See Cap Ex reference below).

Also, how could you compare the Cash Flow of two properties if you include the Debt Service as an expense, when the Debt Service is all about the credit worthiness of the person who got the loan, and has nothing to do with the particular characteristics of the property?

The expenses also do not include Depreciation, since it is not a cash expense, but is an "expense allowance" that allows you to deduct over a period of time what you paid for the property.

However, you do include an expense called Capital Expenditure, referred to as Cap Ex, even if that expense does not actually occur that month. It is a "set-aside" to build up a fund to pay for the Cap Ex when it does occur.

Although most discussions of Cash Flow leave out Cap Ex, you should include it because your Lender will want to see it, and because it is an actual expense that will definitely happen at some point. This is the Cap Ex that I referred to above.

See SECTION 8. CAPITAL EXPENDITURES for an explanation of this.

The key to getting a valuable Calculation of the Cash Flow lies in what you decide to include in the category of "expenses."

See more on that below.

But first, let's clear up a fallacy.

LOAN PROCEEDS AND INTEREST INCOME

Some investors using this Calculation include loan proceeds and interest income in Total Income, in addition to the rents.

If that serves your needs, then do it. But it is not what the Calculation is designed for, and it distorts the results.

I never include loan proceeds, and I never have an investment property that is loaning out money and receiving interest payments.

This measure is all about the property, and the only income considered should be the income from the operation of the property.

Loan proceeds are not income.

And an interest-bearing account is not part of the property; it is where the owner of the property has taken cash flow or income from the operation of the property in the past, or the Cap Ex funds, and put it in an account in his name. So, the interest is not income from the property.

What if someone has a Fourplex for sale, and he told you that the Fourplex had a monthly CF of $3,000 last year, and when you look at the income you see four units renting for $1,000 per month, and a 10% VACL, resulting in $43,200 annual Gross Income. And when you look at expenses you see a total of $31,200. Subtract that, and it leaves a CF of $12,000 and a monthly Cash Flow of $1,000 instead of the $3,000 claimed.

When you ask about the discrepancy, they say, "Oh yeah, I got a loan for $24,000 and that adds $2,000 a month to the Cash Flow."

That's why I don't see any place for loan proceeds in your CF calculation.

Loan proceeds are not Cash Flow from the property; they are debt which must be repaid.

EXPENSES

To repeat, "expenses" as used in Cash Flow analysis, does not include Depreciation and it does not include Debt Service.

It does include an expense called Capital Expenditures, referred to as Cap Ex, which is deducted every month whether there is an actual Cap Ex that month or not.

See SECTION 8. CAPITAL EXPENDITURES for a full explanation.

Basically, Cap Ex is the amount that you have estimated should be set aside each month to cover the occasional major repair, such as a roof, HVAC system, furnace, foundation, or other. It is treated as an actual cash expense each month and accumulated for this purpose.

When you do have an event requiring this major expense, you use the money accumulated for that purpose. You have already been taking it out of the Cash Flow calculations, and now you don't have to. This gives you an even cash flow Calculation over time instead of one that cruises along at a high level and then one day it goes seriously negative and stays that way.

If the fund is not adequate to cover the expense, you get a second lien improvement loan.

The remainder of your expenses for Cash Flow analysis are these.

TAXES. This is Property Taxes. It is a good number to track. Property Taxes are increasing so rapidly across the country that they are turning some positive Cash Flows negative. That could make your property very difficult to sell.

INSURANCE. This is Hazard Insurance, Flood Insurance, and Liability Insurance. If you own investment property through a business entity such as an LLC, which you should, you might consider keeping the insurance coverage as low as possible. Large policies just attract lawsuits, and insurance companies usually refuse to pay a claim anyway, and end up settling for an amount that is probably less than what you have paid them in premiums.

UTILITIES: WATER. Your local government entity might include water, sewer and garbage together in one bill.

UTILITIES: GAS/ELECTRIC.

UTILITIES: SEWER. Your local government entity might include water, sewer, and garbage together in one bill.

UTILITIES: GARBAGE. Your local government entity might include water, sewer, and garbage together in one bill.

REPAIRS.

MANAGEMENT. Whether you include this will depend on your situation. Property management companies typically charge a fee of 10-12% of the monthly rent, plus 50% of the first month's rent when a unit turns over.

VACANCY AND CREDIT LOSS (VACL). If you are projecting expenses on a potential purchase you will use the Gross Potential Income as your cash income number. This number should be 10% of the Gross Potential Income (GPI) from rents. If you are compiling a current Cash Flow Accounting, you should discount the GPI by 5% to arrive at

Gross Operating Income (GOI) because the 5% will represent your actual loss over time because a unit is empty, and use a 5% factor here to reflect the loss or expense that you will incur because of hot checks or reversed bank transfers, or other scams.

BEFORE-TAX AND AFTER-TAX CASH FLOW

Many discussions of Cash Flow will tell you that first you should calculate the Cash Flow before taxes and then determine the amount of taxes and calculate another Cash Flow figure for after taxes.

This is not only a waste of your time, but it is impossible to do.

I have been a Tax Attorney and a Tax Accountant for over 35 years and I can promise you that this function is too complicated to be put into a Calculation with any hope of arriving at a usable number.

And the explanation of why it cannot be done with any accuracy is also too complicated to be attempted here.

CALCULATOR

Once you know your Cash Flow, it is a good idea to Calculate some ratios that will tell you how healthy your investment is in terms of liquidity.

One of those Calculations is the Cash Flow To Total Debt ratio, and here is a Free Calculator to do that.

http://www.danielsoper.com/fincalc/calc.aspx?id=67

- For "Cash flow" enter 37250 (no comma).
- For "Total debt" enter 300000.
- Click "Calculate."

Your Cash Flow To Total Debt Ratio is 12.42%.

Of course, your ratio will improve as you hold the property because the level of your debt will decrease, and, assuming that you are able to raise rents, you Cash Flow will increase.

SECTION 12.

CASH FLOW: DISCOUNTED

Discounted Cash Flow (DCF) is a Calculation of the Present Value (PV) of future streams of cash flow, based on an interest rate used as a discount factor.

It is similar to the Section on Present Value that determines the present value of assets with a known value in the future, but the Discounted Cash Flow Calculation is for a stream of periodic payments.

It is really the inverse of the Compound Interest concept. Instead of adding in interest and interest-on-interest to a present value going into the future, we are pulling out an interest factor and an interest-on-interest factor from a future amount as we bring it back to the present.

Let's assume that you have projected a stream of payments that you expect to result from an investment property, such as Cash Flow.

You have a multi-family property that is creating monthly Cash Flow of $2,400 and you want to know the present value of two years of such payments.

You have placed a time value on the use of money in your life at 12%. In other words, you are willing to pay 12% for the use of other people's money because you know you can make a profit using that money in your business activities. Therefore, the Time Value of Money for you is 12%.

The monthly Interest rate factor of 12% annual interest is 1%.

Let's discount the value of the first twelve months of Cash Flow.

For the first month, the value is $2,400 because you have the money in your hand now, assuming that you collect rents on the first day of the month.

To determine the present value of $2,400 received a month from now, you discount it by the 1% interest rate that you have assigned as your time value of money.

PV = CF ÷ (1 + I), WHERE

PV IS THE PRESENT VALUE,

CF IS THE CASH FLOW AMOUNT, AND

I IS THE INTEREST RATE FACTOR YOU HAVE ASSIGNED TO THE TIME PERIOD.

$$PV = 2{,}400 \div (1 + .01)$$

$$PV = 2{,}400 \div 1.01$$

$$PV = 2{,}376.24$$

So, the Discounted Cash Flow value of the $2,400 that you will receive at the beginning of next month is $2,376.24 today.

To discount the Cash Flow for the third month, the Calculation is slightly different.

PV = CF ÷ (1 + I)^n, WHERE

PV IS THE PRESENT VALUE,

CF IS THE CASH FLOW AMOUNT,

I IS THE INTEREST RATE FACTOR YOU HAVE ASSIGNED, AND

n IS THE NUMBER OF PERIODS YOU ARE DISCOUNTING FOR.

The Calculation is the same as above, except that you are receiving the CF at the beginning of the third month and discounting it back for two months instead of one.

PV = 2,400 ÷ [(1 + .01) (1 + .01)]

PV = 2,400 ÷ (1.01 x 1.01)

PV = 2,400 ÷ 1.0201

PV = 2,352.71

So, your third month Cash Flow of $2,400 has a value today of $2,352.71.

You see the pattern here, so I'll run quickly through the rest.

Fourth: 2,400 ÷ 1.0303 = 2,329.42

Fifth: 2,400 ÷ 1.0406 = 2,306.36

Sixth: 2,400 ÷ 1.051 = 2,283.54

Seventh: 2,400 ÷ 1.0615 = 2,260.95

Eighth: 2,400 ÷ 1.0714 = 2,240.06

Ninth: 2,400 ÷ 1.0828567 = 2,216.36

Tenth: 2,400 ÷ 1.093685 = 2,194.42

Eleventh: 2,400 ÷ 1.104622 = 2,172.69

Twelfth: 2,400 ÷ 1.115668 = 2,151.18

The total amount of the twelve Discounted Cash Flows is $27,583.93.

The undiscounted amount would be 12 x 2,400 = $28,800.

The difference is $1,216.07, which is 4.22% less.

The difference between the stated amount and the discounted amount for the second year of payments would be even less.

If you just look at the 13th Cash Flow amount, you will see.

$$PV = CF \div (1 + I)^n$$

$$PV = 2,400 \div [(1 + .01)(1 + .01)(1 + .01)(1 + .01)(1 + .01)(1 + .01)(1 + .01)(1 + .01)(1 + .01)(1 + .01)(1 + .01)(1 + .01)]$$

$$PV = 2,400 \div (1.01 \times 1.01 \times 1.01 \times 1.01 \times 1.01 \times 1.01 \times 1.01 \times 1.01 \times 1.01 \times 1.01 \times 1.01 \times 1.01)$$

$$PV = 2,400 \div 1.126825$$

$$PV = 2,129.77$$

The Present Value of that $2,400 monthly Cash Flow a year from now is $2,129.77, a difference of $270.23.

Discounted Cash Flow becomes important when you are looking at your Cash on Cash Return (COCR) on your investment.

See SECTION 43. RETURN ON CASH for more information.

COCR = CF ÷ ICI, WHERE

COCR IS YOUR CASH ON CASH RETURN,

CF IS YOUR CASH FLOW FOR THE PERIOD, AND

ICI IS YOUR INITIAL CASH INVESTMENT.

If your ICI was $160,000 for this multi-family property that is producing $28,800 in annual CF:

COCR = CF ÷ ICI

COCR = 28,800 ÷ 160,000

COCR = 18.0

So, your Cash on Cash Return for the first year would be 18.0%.

But since you put all of the $160,000 into the investment up front, and received the Cash Flow over a 12-month period, a more accurate calculation would be to use the Discounted Cash Flow method.

COCR = CF ÷ ICI

COCR = 27,583.93 ÷ 160,000

COCR = 17.24%

This is for the first year. The amount would be lower for the second, and the third, and so forth.

The Discounted Cash Flow method will also give you a better estimate of your Payback Period.

See SECTION 39. PAYBACK PERIOD for more information.

PP = ICI ÷ CF

PP = 160,000 ÷ 2,400

PP = 66.67

The Payback Period is 66.67 months using the undiscounted Cash Flow method. That's five years, six months and 20 days.

To do the same Calculation for Discounted Cash Flow, we would need to know the amount for each month for the same period, add them together, and divide by the total number to get the average, and use that number.

Instead, we'll just use that 13th payment that we calculated above.

PP = ICI ÷ CF

PP = 160,000 ÷ 2,129.77

PP = 75.125

So, just using a single one-year-old Discounted Cash Flow, the Payback Period is pushed out to 6 years, 3 months and 4 days.

There are many reasons for using Discounted Cash Flow when comparing numbers in the present with numbers in the future. You will always get a more accurate Calculation.

CALCULATOR

Now that you understand how to use Discounted Cash Flow, here is a Free Calculator that will do it for you.

https://www.calculatorsoup.com/calculators/financial/present-value-cash-flows-calculator.php

- For "Interest Rate" enter 1 to indicate the monthly rate of 1% that reflects our 12% annual discount rate.

- For "Compounding" enter 1 to indicate that we only want the discount to be applied monthly.

- For "Cash Flow at" select "Beginning" to indicate when in the month the payment is received.

- For "Number of Line" select 10 just for this Example.

- For "Periods" enter 1.

- For "Cash Flow" enter 2,400.

- Click "Calculate."

TCJA FOR REAL ESTATE INVESTORS

You will get a chart showing the Discounted Cash Flow for each of the monthly amounts of $2,400 and a total for all.

Look at Period #10, which represents the tenth month of payments that we are discounting, and you will see that the Discounted Cash Flow is $2,194.42.

This is exactly the same amount that we got in the above Calculation that we did by hand.

So, we did OK.

However, this Calculator can do Calculations that, while I might be able to do them, I would never be able to explain them to you.

For instance, you can use this Calculator to discount future monthly payments that are not even, or that are even, but include something else occasionally such as a principal payment, or a late payment.

You just plug in whatever that amount will be in the appropriate "Period" line.

For this Calculator you only have to make sure that the payments are all at the same interval, and the same discount rate is applied throughout.

SECTION 13.

DEBT SERVICE RATIO

The Debt Service Ratio (DSR) tells you the relationship between the Net Operating Income (NOI) and the amount necessary to service the debt on the property.

DSR = NOI ÷ DS, where

DSR is the Debt Service Ratio,

NOI is the Net Operating Income, and

DS is the Debt Service.

You have a 10-unit Apartment Building and your NOI is $47,500.

You have a $525,000 Mortgage, with monthly payments of $3,150, an annual total of $37,800.

DSR = NOI ÷ DS

DSR = 47,500 ÷ 37,800

DSR = 1.2566

Your Debt Service Ratio is 1.2566, or 125.66%.

Also, this means that after payment of the Mortgage from the Net Operating Income, there will be $9,700 left.

CALCULATOR

The Debt Service Ratio is a fairly simple two-factor Calculation, but if you would like to use a Calculator to do it, here's one:

https://www.ajdesigner.com/php_dcr/debt_coverage_ratio.php

- For "annual net operating income" enter 47500 (no comma).

- For "annual debt service" enter 37800 (no comma).

- Click "Calculate."

Your Debt Service Ratio is 1.2566.

This is the same Calculation that we got above doing it by hand.

SECTION 14.

DEPRECIATION

When a taxpayer buys an investment property such as a Duplex, the money he pays for it is not an expense that can be deducted from the income produced by the property before the taxable income amount is determined.

This is true whether he pays cash for the property or finances the entire amount, or any combination of the two.

Only the interest paid on the loan, if there is a loan, is deductible, because interest is a deductible business expense.

It seems unfair, and maybe it is, but the way the IRS make this unfair situation into a fair situation, and encourages investors to put their money into such projects, is through what is called "Depreciation Allowance," which is usually just referred to as Depreciation.

Depreciation is not an actual out-of-pocket expense, but the taxpayer can deduct it like any other business expense as though it were actually paid, because it is what the IRS considers an "expense allocation."

The IRS claims to have a rational explanation for this. Their position is that during the life of the asset, as the asset is producing income, it will be wearing out. Therefore, the deduction of the amount paid should be taken over the life of the asset, as it wears out, to parallel the production of income by the asset.

It sounds good, but it is difficult to reconcile with another IRS creation, the Section 179 Bonus Depreciation, in which the taxpayer can take an immediate 50% Depreciation Deduction for certain new personal assets purchased for the business. (Ed. Note: this was increased to 100% for both new and used qualifying property by the new Tax Cuts And Jobs Act.)

But let's just take it as it is.

The assets that you purchase and depreciate will have a "life."

The asset "life" is the period of time over which the asset can be depreciated.

It is not the actual life of the asset, but a number assigned by the IRS, just because they are the IRS and they can do whatever they want.

The Depreciation will either be Straight-line Depreciation, or Accelerated Depreciation.

For more information, see SECTION 21. DEPRECIATION: STRAIGHT LINE and SECTION 15. DEPRECIATION: ACCELERATED.

Accelerated Depreciation comes in different forms.

See SECTION 17. DEPRECIATION: DOUBLE DECLINING BALANCE and SECTION 22. DEPRECIATION: 150% DECLINING BALANCE for more information.

Whether your Depreciation is Straight-line or Accelerated will depend on whether it is Section 1250 Property or Section 1245 Property.

See SECTION 20. DEPRECIATION: SECTION 1250 PROPERTY and SECTION 19. DEPRECIATION: SECTION 1245 PROPERTY for more information.

And finally, when you sell the property, the IRS wants the money back.

For more information, see SECTION 23. DEPRECIATION RECAPTURE for more information.

This is an overview of Depreciation.

I have a Section on each type of Depreciation, with an explanation, and an Example worked through. For five of them I also have a Free Calculator for you to try out.

Now that you understand what Depreciation is, go to each of those Sections for the details.

I have made more money by using Depreciation wisely than I have by trying to negotiate the lowest possible prices.

I strongly recommend that you learn everything about Depreciation.

FINAL THOUGHTS

In addition to this book on Tax Cuts And Jobs Act, and the book on 50 Real Estate Investing Calculations, I invite you to consider "How To Do A Section 1031 Like Kind Exchange."

You can do a "Look Inside" for what the book is about, and some good information on real estate investing in general at:

amazon.com/Michael-Lantrip/e/B01N2ZRGUY

Thank You!

TCJA FOR REAL ESTATE INVESTORS

Made in the USA
Coppell, TX
23 January 2021